D0712751

RENE

THE GERMAN ELECTORAL SYSTEM

For Renate, Rich and Chris

The German Electoral System

PETER JAMES
University of Northumbria

ASHGATE

Published by
Ashgate Publishing Limited
Gower House
Croft Road
Aldershot
Hants GU11 3HR
England

Ashgate Publishing Company
Suite 420
101 Cherry Street
Burlington, VT 05401-4405
USA

Ashgate website: http://www.ashgate.com

British Library Cataloguing in Publication Data
James, Peter, 1946 Apr. 18-
    The German electoral system
    1. Germany (Federal Republic) . Bundestag - Elections
    2. Elections - Germany 3. Germany - Politics and government -
    1945-1990 4. Germany - Politics and government - 1990 -
    I. Title
    324.6'3'0943

Library of Congress Cataloging-in-Publication Data
James, Peter, 1946 Apr. 18-
    The German electoral system / Peter James.
        p. cm.
    Includes bibliographical references and index.
    ISBN 0-7546-1740-8
        1. Elections--Germany--History. 2. Representative government and
    representation--Germany--History. 3. Proportional representation--Germany--History. 4.
    Political parties--Law and legislation--Germany--History. I. Title.

    JN3971.A95J36 2004
    324.6'3'0943--dc22

2003056779

ISBN 0 7546 1740 8

Printed and bound in Great Britain by MPG Books Ltd, Bodmin, Cornwall

Contents

List of Figures and Tables

Introduction

The Role of Elections

Free and fair elections are one of the cornerstones of a liberal parliamentary democracy. Any political system which makes some genuine attempt to establish a form of government which corresponds in any real degree to the wishes of the people being governed – preferably the majority of those people – must hold elections to ascertain the people's wishes. The basic function of an election in a democratic society is to provide a means by which the will of the people can be established, recorded and used to elect a body to govern on behalf of the people. That body should represent the various trends of political opinion.

Democracy and elections are closely interwoven. An election is the basis upon which democratic, constitutional procedure rests; its purpose is to offer a mandate to govern for a limited period of time. Without democracy there is no election and without an election no democracy, although an election *per se* does not of course guarantee democracy. There must be an acceptance of the principle of pluralism, so that the majority does not abuse the minority. Power must not be abused.

However, it must be recognised that politics is, fundamentally, a battle for power. On the day of an election that power is transferred briefly to the voters. The act of participation by the voter allows him or her to take part in the decision-making process. Intentional non-participation (abstention) is also a way of influencing the situation, because, of course, turnout at an election can affect the result. The politicians know this and they know too that, if they want to be re-elected, they must take the ordinary citizens' opinions and wishes into consideration, since it is the voters who play a key role in the distribution of that power.

In this way it is essential for politicians to grasp the fact that any power they are granted by the people is for a limited time only. In any democratic system today's government can become tomorrow's Opposition. Political parties should never forget that any democratically elected government has been elected to rule on behalf of all the people, with their consent, and for a restricted period. A strict check is kept on any elected government, not only by the parliamentary body chosen at the original election, but also by the voters, who, if dissatisfied, have the power to change things at the next election.

Elections not only give citizens the right to pass judgement and to express their political views, they also legitimise power and keep a check on the people's political representatives. Whilst in any democratic system the majority view prevails, it is a fundamental principle in a liberal parliamentary democracy that the minority must not be suppressed or exploited in any way. In a political system based on human rights and the rule of law, minorities and minority views must be respected and protected at all times. The basic functions and essential characteristics of elections include that of representation. The deputies, or members of parliament, who have been elected must strive to represent *all* the voters they represent, regardless of how they voted. In this way important aspects, namely those of competition and potential changes in democratic power, are guaranteed by the election process.

When it comes to the method of voting adopted in a constitutional democracy, an electoral system can be viewed as a way of translating the people's votes into seats in parliament, or in whatever body is chosen to represent the people. Five principles can be identified. Firstly, an electoral system should provide a parliament that reflects the main trends of opinion within the electorate. Secondly, it should provide government based on the wishes of the electorate. Thirdly, it should provide for the election of representatives who are qualified for government and who are capable of forming meaningful links between themselves and the people they represent. Fourthly, it should provide a situation which favours the formation of a government capable of governing effectively. Fifthly, it could be argued that ideally an electoral system should also provide an equilibrium of social forces which simultaneously reconcile unity and diversity. These five principles need to be taken together, so that no single consideration can completely override the others.

In his book on empirical electoral research, Dieter Roth, Head of the German electoral research institute, *Forschungsgruppe Wahlen* in Mannheim, states that fundamentally electoral systems have two main aims: firstly, the production of workable government majorities, and secondly, the establishment of a parliament which is as accurate a reflection as possible of society.[1]

All this gives rise to a key question: do electoral systems shape political systems or vice versa? Some eminent experts, for example the German political scientist Karl-Rudolf Korte, view the electoral system as being not only central to the power struggle in politics but also as being influenced by the structure of the party system, the stability of the governmental system and political culture.[2] The type of political parties which emerge and the nature of a country's party system can, and will, influence its electoral system.

However, the opposite can also be true. The American author David P. Conradt states in his respected standard work *The German Polity* that 'most political scientists and political leaders assume that the electoral law will affect the character and structure of its party system and hence its politics'.[3] In a British context the adoption of a proportional/additional member electoral system at the end of the twentieth century for the newly created Scottish and Welsh parliaments demonstrated that an electoral system can influence a political system. This point was made to the author in an interview with Prof. Charlie Jeffery, the Deputy Director of the Institute for German Studies in April 2002.[4] So, as far as this fundamental question is concerned, there is clearly some interaction in a two-way process.

There are of course other factors in a country's political system which also play a part in this respect. For example, in postwar Germany the introduction of a constructive vote of no confidence in the 1949 constitution made a substantial contribution to political stability, after the chaotic political circumstances of the Weimar Republic. Nevertheless the electoral system itself, via the way in which it acts as a mechanism for allocating parliamentary seats, can influence the way the results of an election are interpreted, and this in turn may affect the nature and development of the party system. For an example of the difference that the application of a different electoral system to the same set of results can make, see Table 1.1 in Chapter 1.

In the case of Germany, the fact that the Federal Republic adopted an electoral system based on proportional representation, with an all-important cut-off clause (the 5 per cent hurdle), definitely influenced the development of the party system. As will be seen later in this book, the tightening of the electoral hurdle was initially largely responsible for the concentration of the West German party system between 1949, when 11 parties entered the *Bundestag* in Bonn, and 1961, by which time a three-party system had been established. Although the two main parties (the CDU/CSU and the SPD) established themselves as the major players in the (West) German party system (and they still play the dominant role in German politics today), the German electoral system gave considerable power and influence to a third party, the tiny FDP. The German liberal party found itself in the unaccustomed role of opposition party in the *Bundestag* in Berlin after the 1998 federal elections, the German Green Party, a similarly small but now also influential party, to a certain extent began to take over from the FDP as the third party at federal level, as it offered its services as a government coalition partner to the SPD.

Owing to the German tradition of the frequent formation of coalition governments at both national and regional level, it was *not* the two major parties that simply took it in turns to rule alone as the single government party, as in the USA or the UK. Both of those countries have a different electoral system from Germany, and there can be little doubt that this affected the development of the American and British party systems. It is also quite clear that in the case of the Federal Republic of Germany the electoral system has also had a demonstrable effect on the party system.

Notes

1   Dieter Roth (1998), *Empirische Wahlforschung*, Opladen: Leske und Budrich, p. 212.
2   Karl-Rudolf Korte (1998), *Wahlen in der BRD*, Bonn: Bundeszentrale für politische Bildung, p. 20.
3   David P. Conradt (2001) *The German Polity*, 7th edn, New York: Longman, p. 147.
4   Interview with Prof. Charlie Jeffery, Deputy Director of the Institut für Deutschlandstudien on 11 April 2002.

Chapter 1

The Historical Dimension

The current German electoral system has of course been developed from, and influenced by, political experiences in Germany's past.

1.1 The Prussian Electoral System 1849–71 (1918)

Even before the diverse German states were first unified in 1871, an electoral system existed in the dominant state, Prussia, under Otto von Bismarck. This was significant, since Bismarck and Prussia not only played a leading role in the first unification of Germany but also continued to dominate the new German nation afterwards, in terms of population, area and power. Under the political system of the Second Empire from 1871 until 1918 the King of Prussia was also German Emperor. Although each of the German states had its own electoral system, Prussia was extremely influential and it retained approximately the same system up until 1918.

Voting rights in many areas of the German Second Empire were based on the principles of hard work, the ownership of property, and above all tax contributions. The Prussian electoral system, known in German as the *Dreiklassenwahlrecht*, divided the electorate into three classes. It was first introduced on 30 May 1849. The system was not universal (it excluded anyone who received alms), it was unequal and indirect.

Under the Prussian system, first of all *Wahlmänner* (representatives) were chosen; these were the people who actually cast the votes on behalf of the voters, along the lines of a type of electoral college in the USA. There was one of these representatives for every 250 people, and they were elected by an absolute majority, i.e. one candidate had to obtain over 50 per cent of the vote, and, if necessary, a second ballot was held with the two leading candidates from the first round standing again. The original voting wards in those days contained between 750 and 1,750 people; this meant that each ward was represented by between three and six representatives. Since Prussia was at that time by far the largest of the German states, it contained a large number of electoral wards. In 1908, for example, Prussia had 29,028 wards.[1]

The Prussian electoral system divided the electorate into three classes according to the amount of taxes paid. The first class contained very few people. They were the richest, most powerful citizens who owned the most property and paid the highest taxes. The second class contained the middle group, who were reasonably well-off, owned some property and therefore paid taxes, but did not contribute as much as those in class one. The third class, or category, covered everyone else. Class three did offer voting rights to people who paid no taxes at all, but excluded those who received charity in the form of alms.

Although the three classes were of vastly differing sizes, each class elected one third of the deputies to the Prussian parliament. Each class also selected from within its own ranks – i.e. those eligible to vote – an equal number (either one or two) of representatives (*Wahlmänner*). They were responsible for actually casting the votes on behalf of the people they represented. By present-day standards, this was not a very democratic or 'fair' system, especially given the huge discrepancy in size between the three groups of voters.

The Prussian three-class electoral system divided its voters for the election of 1850 as follows: class one contained 4.7 per cent of the electorate, class two 12.6 per cent and class three 82.7 per cent. In other words 153,000 voters in class one had equal voting rights with 2,691,000 in class three, because each class elected one third of the deputies in the Prussian parliament. In 1903 the same system gave 239,000 electors in class one the same amount of influence as 6,006,000 in class three. So at the 1903 election the Conservatives, who gained 324,157 votes, obtained 143 deputies in the Prussian parliament, whilst the Social Democrats, with 314,149 votes, obtained no deputies. At the 1908 elections in Prussia the Conservatives were allocated 152 seats in parliament in return for their 354,785 votes, but the Social Democrats received only seven seats in return for 598,522 votes.[2]

For the 1908 election the territory of Prussia was divided into some 29,000 wards, each containing at least 750 people, who were then put into one of three classes according to taxes paid. Each class then cast its votes via its *Wahlmänner* (there were between three and six for each ward) for its constituency, of which there were 276. Each constituency elected not just one deputy but between one and three deputies. This was another means of manipulation.

Women did not have the right to vote, as they were neither taxpayers nor property owners. Under the Prussian electoral system four-fifths of the (male) electorate were able to elect only one third of the deputies at most elections. This was due to the fact that class three often contained around 80 per cent of the electorate. The Prussian electoral law of 1860 did not take population changes into account or revise electoral boundaries.

It is worth remembering that this electoral system affected most Germans up until 1918, owing to Prussia's dominant position even after unification in 1871. In 1910, for example, Prussia contained over 60 per cent of the population of the German *Reich*.[3] Rokkan Stein commented that it would be difficult to devise an electoral measure more calculated to alienate the lower classes from the national political system than the one promulgated in Prussia in 1849.[4]

1.2 The Second Empire

In 1867 Bismarck, after the victory against Austria the previous year, established the North German Confederation and a parliament, the *Reichstag*, was elected on 1 July 1867. Bismarck granted universal suffrage, with direct and secret voting rights, to all males over twenty-five for that election. This arrangement was adopted for the German Second Empire. However, elections during the period 1871–1918 were held on working days and the introduction of a secret ballot did not necessarily mean, in practice, an end to intimidation, since the regulations continued to vary from one German state to another. Prussia, the largest and most powerful state, retained open voting in elections to its state assembly right up until 1918.

National elections to the *Reichstag* were based on single-member constituencies, with deputies having to gain an absolute majority of the vote in their constituencies. Second ballots were often required, if no candidate gained over 50 per cent in the first round of voting. In 1873 the national parliament (*Reichstag*) consisted of 397 deputies, one from each of the electoral districts in Germany. This meant that, on average, each parliamentary deputy represented about 100,000 people. Each German state had to have at least one representative. There were, however, wide variations in both the size of the individual German states and the type of electoral system used.

For example, the state of Württemberg in 1910 contained less than 4 per cent of the German population. It operated a secret and direct system of voting, with 69 deputies being elected via its constituencies and 23 via proportional representation. In the German state of Schaumburg-Lippe two deputies were appointed by the monarch, one was elected by the clergy, one by a group of professors, three by the cities and seven by the rural communities.[5]

In many states landowners and taxpayers were extremely privileged whilst in other states membership of religious denominations affected franchise.

Despite the fact that each state had its own electoral system, the official position remained that the electoral law, laid down in the constitutions of the North German Federation on 12 January 1867 (provisional) and for the North German Parliament on 31 May 1869, was adopted in 1871 as the model for the Second Empire, valid until the end of the First World War. The 1:2 ratio of urban to rural life, which existed when the German Empire was founded, had been reversed by 1918. That had, however, not been reflected at all by any constituency boundary changes.

Both the North German Confederation and the Second Empire had an upper chamber (*Bundesrat*) consisting of delegates sent by the states – usually selected by the Prince (*Fürst*) or someone appointed by him – plus a lower chamber (*Reichstag*), elected by all male citizens over 25. Anyone entitled to vote was also entitled to stand for election. Excluded from the right to vote were those placed in care or in a state of bankruptcy, those who had lost their citizenship following a court sentence and anyone receiving alms. Each voter had one vote, recorded in secret, and the successful candidate was elected by an absolute majority. That meant that sometimes of course a second ballot was required and, in the event of a tie, lots were drawn. When a deputy left parliament a new election was held to find a replacement, along the lines of a present-day by-election in Great Britain. From 1871 to 1918 Germany was divided into 397 constituencies, each with an average population of around 100,000.

During the Second Empire Germany's Social Democratic Party (SPD) was not treated very fairly, partly due to the constituency boundaries being out of date. To give just one example of how the Social Democrats suffered, at the 1912 *Reichstag* election 7,706 votes were enough to elect a Conservative candidate in the constituency of Heiligenbeil/Pr.Eylau, yet in the constituency of Bochum 53,333 votes were not enough to give the Social Democrat candidate victory.[6]

Under the Prussian three-class system sometimes less than 10 per cent of the electorate voted, but participation gradually increased as time went on in the Second Empire. However the system favoured the Conservatives and the National Liberals, as well as the Centre Party (*Zentrum*) and even some minority groups. Despite voting rights being increased in general terms, the Social Democrats continued to be disadvantaged, because the considerable increase in their share of the vote was not reflected in a corresponding increase in parliamentary seats. Consequently they began to campaign for some form of proportional representation rather than a majority electoral system.

1.3 The Weimar Republic 1919–33 (1945)

On 30 November 1918 a decree was passed stating that elections to the German National Assembly, to be elected on 19 January 1918, would take place on the basis of proportional representation. This was partly because of the way in which the electoral system of the German Empire had completely ignored the rural/urban changes (*Landflucht*) when drawing up constituency boundaries, and it was of course also partly a response to the way in which the Prussian three-class system had unfairly favoured a small conservative upper class in the population.

In the Weimar Republic, Germany's first attempt at establishing a democratic system, bankrupts were no longer deprived of their voting rights, elections had to be held on a Sunday or public holiday, the voting age was lowered from 25 to 20, and women were given the vote for the first time in German history, according to the Weimar electoral law (*Reichswahlgesetz*) of 27 April 1920.

The existing large number (397) of small constituencies was reduced to just 35 large ones (the two Württemberg constituencies were joined and Alsace-Lorraine was occupied by the French), in which there was one parliamentary seat for every 60,000 voters. That meant that the number of seats in parliament following an election depended on the turnout at the election. The number of deputies in the *Reichstag* during the Weimar Republic in fact fluctuated between 459 in 1920 and 647 in 1933. In 1928, for instance, a 78.8 per cent turnout produced 493 members of the German parliament, whilst the 1930 national election, with a turnout of 82 per cent, meant that 577 deputies entered the *Reichstag*.[7] Any residue of votes cast for a party over and above the 60,000 required for a seat in parliament was added to any remaining totals, in order to try to make up enough votes to gain another seat: if a party had 30,000 or more votes remaining, it was awarded a final seat.

Essentially the Weimar voter was selecting a party rather than a candidate, since the party lists were firmly fixed before the election and the order of the candidates on those lists could not be altered (*starre Listen*). Any voter who was not a member of a political party had no way of influencing the choice of candidates. Neither could he or she influence the order of the candidates on the list, which in fact determined their chances of success.

Weimar's political system included a bicameral legislature, attaching greater importance to the lower house of parliament, the *Reichstag*, than the upper house, the *Reichsrat*. The original electoral law, passed in April 1920 and amended in March 1924, was intended to represent the wishes of the people as fairly as possible via a system of pure proportionality. Laudable though this aim was in theory, in practice it led to a multiplicity of parties entering parliament. In fact a total of 41 parties contested the 1928 Weimar elections and in 1930 there were 32 parties on the political stage, of which 14 gained parliamentary seats.[8] Throughout the history of the Weimar Republic no single party ever gained an absolute majority in the *Reichstag* – not even the NSDAP in or after 1933. Between 1919 and 1930 there were 16 governments with an average period of office of just eight months each.

It is important to remember that the Weimar voters were able to influence politics in two other ways: firstly, they could directly elect the President of the Republic, and secondly, they could vote in plebiscites. However the Weimar electoral system clearly encouraged multi-party parliaments, with too many splinter parties, and it was not conducive to the formation of stable governments. The presence of numerous small parties meant that they were not forced to compromise or integrate in promoting political stability.

A constitution can establish a theoretical framework, within which a democratic system may flourish, but educating the people who live under that system is not always an easy or immediate process. The social, economic and psychological aspects of the special set of circumstances following Germany's defeat after the First World War affected the political system of the Weimar Republic and certainly contributed to its downfall. Several experts have expressed the opinion that, under such circumstances, it is unlikely that a different electoral system alone would have changed the fate of the Weimar period or have prevented the rise to power of Hitler and the National Socialists.

So a system of pure PR, whilst a great improvement on its predecessors, was not the complete answer. A party with only 2 per cent support was allocated 2 per cent of the seats in parliament and that did little to strengthen or stabilise the Weimar democracy. Unfortunately, neither did the direct election (for seven years) of a President of the Republic, nor the direct power afforded to the electorate by means of plebiscites. Although the latter was based on the 1874 Swiss model (in theory a first-class contribution to democracy), in practice it was unable to make up for the inherent weaknesses of a democracy which contained too few democrats and a republic which contained too few republicans.

Professor Peter Pulzer also reminds us that 'all research into electoral systems has shown … [that] all systems distort the intention of the voter to some degree'.[9] In this way, then, even the pure proportionality of Weimar's political system did not guarantee perfection by any means.

Although the rule of the Weimar Republic was not officially terminated until 1945, in practice its constitution was suspended with the Enabling Act (*Ermächtigungsgesetz*) on 24 March 1933, after Hitler had come to power on 30 January 1933. In the new situation which obtained under National Socialism, where the fundamental will to make a democratic system work was lacking, the electoral system became as irrelevant as the elections themselves.

So it would be incorrect to assert that the Weimar electoral system was a major factor in getting the NSDAP into power, even though there is a sense in which a totally proportional system can enable a party to win parliamentary seats when it still represents only a minority of the electorate. In fact gaining a few seats between 1924 and 1928 was not really a major factor in Hitler's rise to power. Once public opinion had turned towards the Nazi party offering a 'place in the sun' to a German nation suffering a crisis of mass unemployment and galloping inflation, a majority electoral system would probably have resulted in a landslide victory.

Remarkably, the National Socialists could not attain an absolute majority of the vote even in March 1933. Despite the fact that by then Hitler was already the German Chancellor and despite the fact that the SS and SA were already well into their stride, the NSDAP gained a 'mere' 43.9 per cent of the popular vote. Although some observers point to the existence of manipulation even then, the 1933 elections to the *Reichstag* are sometimes regarded as the last free elections in Germany before the end of the Second World War.

1.4 Discussions on a New Electoral System 1945–49

When Germany was setting out to make a fresh start after unconditional surrender in 1945, the first local elections held in the American and French zones of occupation were conducted under the old Weimar system, but in the British zone a compromise between that and the British majority method was adopted, as an attempt to introduce an element of personal choice of candidate. Those local elections did, to a certain extent, set some sort of precedent. However, a number of other factors also influenced the debates in the Parliamentary Council, which took place between the autumn of 1948 and the spring of 1949, on what sort of electoral system to adopt for a new West German state. The tyranny of the 12 years of Nazi dictatorship and the failure of the Weimar political system, with elections based on pure proportional representation, were of course not the least important of these factors.

At least the prevailing circumstances that obtained when the western part of Germany was making a second attempt to establish a democratic political system were better than those that obtained after the First World War. The Nazi experience had finally eradicated Germany's imperial past and with it the traditional social and political values of a bygone era. Prussia had ceased to exist.

The Parliamentary Council, which sat from September 1948 until May 1949, consisted of 65 members, under the chairmanship of Konrad Adenauer: 27 members each from the CDU/CSU and the SPD, five from the FDP, and two each from the communist KPD, the Centre Party (*Zentrum*), and the DP (*Deutsche Partei*). Although there are many different possible electoral systems, at the time only two major systems were under serious consideration: a relative majority system, along the lines of the British system (favoured by the CDU/CSU) or a system of PR (favoured by the SPD). Many of the champions of a proportional method of voting wanted to combine it with a personalised element, which would allow the selection of individual candidates, as well as parties.

1.5 Majority System versus Proportional Representation

In a majority electoral system the electoral area is divided into constituencies, in which each party or independent group puts forward a candidate. The voter normally has one vote only. The candidate who gains a majority of the votes is elected. This majority can be an absolute majority, i.e. the candidate who attains over 50 per cent of the votes. If no single candidate achieves this in the first round, then a second ballot is held, sometimes with only the two candidates with the highest vote standing again, as happened in the German Second Empire. A qualified majority may be stipulated, for example requiring the winning candidate to obtain two thirds or three quarters of the total votes cast.

A simple, or relative, majority requires the winner to obtain more votes (even if it is only one more vote) than any other candidate. Under this system, applied in Great Britain and the United States, it frequently happens that more voters in a constituency vote *against* than *for* the winning candidate, because their votes are distributed amongst two or more other candidates. For example, in a constituency where 60,000 votes are cast, 28,000 (less than half) might have been gained by the winning candidate, whilst the second and third candidates gained 20,000 and 12,000 respectively. In this 'winner takes all' system there are no prizes (in fact no recognition whatsoever) for coming second.

In two British general elections since 1945 (1951 and February 1974) the party which was elected to govern actually gained fewer votes than the one which went into opposition. Similar situations have occurred in the USA, and the highly controversial 2000 presidential election caused some major dissatisfaction amongst the American electorate, producing calls for a change in election methods.

Many people consider that an electoral system based on proportional representation (PR) can sometimes offer a more accurate reflection of the wishes of the electorate. The following example shows how the application of two different electoral systems – a PR and a majority (first-past-the-post) system – to the same set of results can produce a substantial difference in the allocation of parliamentary seats.

Supposing in an electoral area three competing parties, A, B and C, gained 36,000, 24,000 and 12,000 votes respectively. If 12 deputies or representatives were to be chosen for that area, under a system of PR party A would receive six, party B four and party C two deputies. This would be a 'fair' or representative/ proportional distribution, based directly on the wishes of the voters. However, under a simple majority system, it could easily happen that party A wins nine out of the 12 constituencies, party B none, and party C three, although twice as many people voted for party B as party C, as shown below:

Table 1.1[10] **First past the post**

Constituency	Party A	Party B	Party C
1	3,400	2,000	600
2	3,300	1,900	700
3	3,000	2,100	800
4	3,400	1,900	700
5	3,500	2,000	600
6	3,600	2,000	400
7	2,900	2,800	300
8	3,700	1,700	700
9	3,400	1,800	1,000
10	1,900	2,000	2,100
11	1,900	1,900	2,000
12	2,000	1,900	2,100
Total	36,000	24,000	12,000

1.6   The Details of Federal Electoral Law

In post-war Germany, in the three western zones of occupation, a committee for electoral matters voted against adopting a simple majority voting system by five votes to three. Both an absolute majority system and a system of pure PR, as adopted for the political system of the Weimar Republic, were rejected unanimously. The need for a strong relationship between a constituency member of parliament and his or her constituents was acknowledged during the discussions of the Parliamentary Council. In 1949 there were 242 constituencies; this was changed to 248 in 1965. With German Unity in 1990 the new enlarged Germany contained 328 constituencies. A further change was adopted for the 2002 federal election, for which the number of constituencies was reduced to 299.

Partly as a consequence of this, the actual number of members of the *Bundestag*, whether in Bonn or Berlin, fluctuated. In 1949 there were 402 deputies, in 1953 there were 487, in 1957 a total of 497 and 499 in 1961. Following the federal elections of 1965, 1969, 1972 and 1976 there were 496 deputies in the German parliament, with 497 in both 1980 and 1987, and 498 in 1983. After the increase in territory in the New Germany in 1990 there should have been a total of 656 representatives in the new *Bundestag*; in practice, however, there were more than that, owing to some additional mandates (see 2.2). The figures for the total number of members of parliament for 1990, 1994, 1998 and 2002 were actually 662, 672, 669 and 603 respectively.

In one of its plenary sessions in 1949 the Council agreed that the form of electoral system to be used in the new West German state would not be laid down in the constitution, i.e. the Basic Law (*Grundgesetz*), but would be left to individual future governments to elucidate by means of federal law. That decision was taken before the draft of the new constitution was handed to the Allies on 8 May 1949. On 10 May 1949 the first federal law, to be valid for the first federal elections in August 1949 only, was put forward; it came into effect on 15 June 1949.

In fact the first federal electoral law contained the expected compromise regarding the voting system to be used. It put forward a mixed system, later to be known as a 'personalised proportional system', whereby a basically proportional method would try to reflect the wishes of the electorate as accurately as possible, whilst still allowing a vote to be cast for an individual candidate in a constituency. In fact the West German voter was given only one vote in 1949 (see below), but that changed four years later, and from the 1953 federal elections right up to the present day every German voter has always had two votes at his or her disposal.

Article 38 of the Basic Law [Art. 38 GG (1)] stated that elections were universal (*allgemein*), direct (*unmittelbar*), free (*frei*), equal (*gleich*) and secret (*geheim*). Universal voting rights means that all German citizens over the age of 18,[11] who fulfil the general requirements, are eligible to vote, regardless of gender, race, religion, or any social, political or economic considerations. Direct means that members of parliament are elected directly, with no intermediate stage involving any sort of Electoral College, in which representatives cast votes on behalf of the voters. Free means that no-one may be subjected to pressure or undue influence when deciding how to vote. Each voter must be free to decide as he or she wishes, without anyone being able to instruct them or know how they voted. Neither may they be forced to vote (voting is not compulsory) or disadvantaged as a result of the way he or she voted. Equal means that all votes carry equal weight; factors such as social status, property owned or taxes paid have no relevance; the only exception to this is that votes cast for parties that do not clear the 5 per cent hurdle are disregarded in the allocation of parliamentary seats. Secret means that it is not permitted for anyone to know how any individual votes are cast. Clearly it is essential to have a secret ballot, if you are also going to have a free vote, where the threat of intimidation and influence are to be eliminated.

It is often forgotten nowadays, but in fact the first electoral law gave the German voter in the 1949 federal elections only one vote each. Sixty per cent of the deputies to be elected to the first *Bundestag* were chosen by a simple majority system in single-member constituencies; the other 40 per cent were chosen on the basis of proportional representation via party lists. A cross was placed against a constituency candidate's name, and it was assumed that the voters were also giving their list vote to the party to which the candidate belonged.

The cut-off clause, in order to try to avoid a multiplicity of parties entering parliament, as had happened during the Weimar Republic, stated that only parties which gained at least 5 per cent of the valid votes in any of the West German *Länder* would qualify for seats in parliament. The alternative way of qualifying for parliamentary representation was to gain a constituency seat. Owing to the fact that at the first federal elections in 1949 the 5 per cent hurdle applied to any *Land*, parties which had strong support in just one federal state – for example the Bavarian Party – entered the Bundestag in Bonn, even though they were virtually unknown outside Bavaria and had no support in West Germany as a whole. As a result, 11 parties were represented in the federal parliament after the first elections.

1.6.1   The Second Law Tightens the Hurdle

Since the first electoral law had been valid for the first federal elections only, another law had to be passed on 8 July 53 for the 1953 federal elections. There were three important changes. Firstly, the voter was given two votes: one for a constituency candidate and one for a party. Secondly, the 60/40 ratio was amended to 50/50, electing one half of the members of parliament from the constituencies (first vote) and the other half via the party lists (second vote). Thirdly, the 5 per cent threshold applied from 1953 onwards to the whole of the Federal Republic, not simply to any *Land*. This change was of crucial importance, since it meant in practice that the number of parties which entered the *Bundestag* was reduced from 11 in 1949 to six after the 1953 federal elections. The alternative to gaining at least 5 per cent of the second (party list) votes in the FRG was still winning one constituency.

1.6.2   The Third Law is Introduced

Before the 1957 federal elections a third federal electoral law was passed, on 7 May 1956. This was not as hurried as the other two laws and was the first one to imply a more permanent status. It was followed in May 1957 with a statement of regulations governing federal elections (*Bundeswahlordnung*). At that time in West Germany voters still had to be aged 21 (the voting age was reduced to 18 in 1970), and aged 25 to stand for election (now also 18). However, the alternative to clearing the 5 per cent clause was changed in 1957 to gaining no longer one, but three direct, i.e. first-vote, constituency seats. That change has remained right up to the present day. The 'three constituency' rule was particularly relevant for the post-1990 federal elections, including the 2002 poll (see 6.1).

At the 1957 federal elections this regulation was manipulated via the use of an electoral agreement between the CDU and the tiny DP (*Deutsche Partei*). The Federal Chancellor Konrad Adenauer (CDU) did this by not putting forward a CDU candidate in certain constituencies. He asked CDU supporters in those constituencies to give their first votes to the DP candidate and their second votes to the CDU on the party list. The 1957 results (in round figures) in Celle in Lower Saxony, for example, demonstrated this clearly. First votes: DP constituency candidate 40,000 (elected), SPD 31,200 (no CDU candidate). Second votes: CDU 38,600, SPD 28,700, DP 14,500.

In this way Adenauer managed to get 17 DP deputies into parliament in Bonn at the 1957 federal elections, although the party gained only 3.4 per cent of the second votes overall. Adenauer did this because he wanted to include certain members of the DP in his coalition government, even though their party was unable to gain enough support from the German voters to clear the 5 per cent hurdle.

The three-constituency regulation was then largely forgotten about until the federal election in 1994. The PDS (Party of Democratic Socialism), which had entered the *Bundestag* for the first time following the 1990 all-German elections, was unable to clear the 5 per cent clause. It gained 4.4 per cent of the second votes in the new, united Germany, but managed to win four constituencies, all in East Berlin. As a result, the PDS entered the *Bundestag* in 1994, with the status of a *Bundestagsgruppe*. The PDS was allocated 4.4 per cent of the total parliamentary seats, on the basis of having won at least three constituencies. The party regained the full status of a *Fraktion*, or parliamentary party, following the 1998 federal elections, when it not only won the same four constituencies in East Berlin but also gained 5.1 per cent of the second valid votes. In a very tense and close-fought election in 2002 the PDS failed to enter the federal parliament, since the party could not clear the 5 per cent hurdle (4 per cent) and won only two constituencies.

Notes

1 For details see *Staatsbürgerliche Arbeitsmappe*, Berlin: Erich Schmidt Verlag, and Mappe 1.
2 Ibid. All figures taken from Mappe 1.
3 Ibid. Mappe 1 gives the figure as 61.9 per cent.
4 Rokkan Stein (1962) in an article 'The Comparative Study of Political Participation: Notes Towards a Perspective on Current Research', in A. Ranney (ed.), *Essays on the Behavioural Study of Politics*, New York: University of Illinois Press, p. 76.
5 See Derek W. Urwin's (1974) article *Germany* in Richard Rose (ed.), *Electoral Behaviour: A Comparative Handbook*, New York: Macmillan, p. 117.
6 Op. cit. *Staatsbürgerkundliche Arbeitsmappe*, Mappe 1.
7 Alfred Milatz (1965), *Wähler und Wahlen in der Weimarer Republik*, Heft 66, Bonn: der Schriftenreihe der Bundeszentrale für politische Bildung.
8 Op. cit. Urwin, p. 112.
9 Peter Pulzer (1983), 'Democracy and the Party System in Weimar Germany', in Vernon Bogdanor and David Butler (eds), *Democracy and Elections. Electoral Systems and their Politic al Consequences*, Cambridge: Cambridge University Press, pp. 84–109.
10 Table taken from Alfred Jüttner (1970), *Wahlen und Wahlrechtsprobleme*, Munich: Olzog.
11 The voting age was reduced from 21 to 18 in 1970.

Chapter 2

The Current Federal Electoral System Emerges

2.1 Development of the (West) German Electoral System

The current electoral system used for federal or national elections to the German federal parliament (*Bundestag*), now situated in the *Reichstag* building in Berlin, is fundamentally the one used in West Germany from 1949 until 1990, the year when the two Germanys – East and West – were reunited. Berlin has been the capital of Germany again since German Unity in 1990 and the seat of government since 1999. The new, united Germany was organised into 328 constituencies. That meant an enlarged *Bundestag* with 656 members, plus any additional mandates (*Überhangmandate*) (see 2.2). In an attempt to reduce the number of parliamentarians in the federal parliament, the 328 constituencies became 299 for the 2002 federal election, which had the effect of reducing the total number of members of parliament (*Abgeordnete*) in Berlin to 598, plus the five additional mandates which occurred (see below).

The electoral system which emerged in 1949 for the newly founded state of West Germany (the Federal Republic of Germany), was used to elect its lower house of parliament (the *Bundestag*) in Bonn, the temporary capital (*die provisorische Hauptstadt*). The method of voting was, as we have seen, based on the principle of proportional representation (PR). For the first national election in 1949 the West German voter had only one vote. From 1953 onwards (see 1.6) however, each voter was given two votes. For this reason the (West) German electoral system used in a national/federal election (*eine Bundestagswahl*) has been described as a 'personalised' system of PR, based on the fact that each voter was, and still is, able to cast two votes. This compromise system meant that the voter was able to vote for both a person, that is, an individual constituency candidate, as well as a political party.

The first vote (*Erststimme*) is cast for a constituency candidate to represent the voter in the area in which he or she lives; the winner was chosen on a simple majority, or first-past-the-post system, as in Great Britain or the United States of America. The second vote (*Zweitstimme*) is cast for a political party on a party list, put forward for that particular federal state (*Landesliste*). With

the second vote, however, the voters have no way of influe
candidates will represent them, as it is the parties who se
and decide the all-important order in which their names ;
lists in each of the federal states (*Bundesländer*).

When it was first designed in 1948/49, the electoral ;
a proportional one, in terms of 'fair' representation. In general terms, that
aim was achieved; the electoral system today is still based on proportional
representation, because if 40 per cent of those who vote in a particular *Land*
voted for a particular party, then that party is allocated 40 per cent of the
Bundestag seats available in that *Land*.

Only parties which gained at least 5 per cent of the valid second votes
– in 1949 in any federal state then, from 1953 onwards, 5 per cent in the
whole of the FRG (see 1.6) – were eligible for parliamentary seats. *Die
Fünfprozentklausel* or *Hürde*, the 5 per cent clause or hurdle, was intentionally
introduced in 1949 as a stabilising factor, after the negative experiences of
the Weimar Republic, which had no cut-off clause in its electoral system. On
one occasion that resulted in 14 parties – out of a total of 32 which contested
the 1930 elections – entering the *Reichstag*, with the ensuing problems and
splintering (*Zersplitterung*) of the party system (see 1.3).

In West Germany the new electoral system, with its 5 per cent clause,
intended of course to avoid such political chaos, which during the Weimar
polity had often resulted in a plethora of splinter parties and the formation of
unstable governments. The new electoral system achieved that aim, in general
terms, although parties which gained 4.9 per cent of the second votes under
the new postwar system might not always have agreed that they should have
been excluded.

There was of course, and still is, an alternative to clearing the 5 per cent
hurdle. If any party won a (first-vote) constituency seat – in 1956 the rule was
changed to at least three constituency seats – then that party was allocated
parliamentary seats, on a proportional basis, in line with the percentage of
second votes it had gained, even if that figure was below 5 per cent (see 1.6).
Ever since the federal election (*Bundestagswahl*) of 1953 half the seats in the
German parliament have been distributed via the direct, first-vote constituency
results, and the other half via the second-vote party list results.

In allocating seats in the *Bundestag* it is the voters' second votes which
are counted first. This determines the number of deputies in parliament
due to a particular party from each *Land*. Since the leader of the largest
party becomes Federal Chancellor, the second vote is the decisive one (*die
Zweitstimme ist wahlentscheidend*). If 120 seats are to be allocated for that

ueral state, and a party – for example the SPD – gains 40 per cent, via the second votes, then the SPD will be allocated 48 seats. Then the number of candidates from the SPD who won their constituencies, via the first votes, is subtracted from 48. If 20 constituencies have already been won by the SPD, only 28 list seats will be allocated.

It is at this stage that the order of the candidates' names on the party list is crucial, since, in our example, the candidate whose name has been placed as number twenty-nine on the party list will not gain a mandate. The ordinary German voter does not know which names are on the party lists, beyond the first five names, which appear on the ballot paper. Neither does the voter have any say on the order in which they appear on those lists. That is determined by the parties. With their second vote voters are simply placing a cross against the name of a political party.

2.2 Additional Mandates (*Überhangmandate*)

It sometimes happens that a party wins all, or nearly all, the constituency seats in a *Land*. Since a constituency seat must always be retained, it could be the case that a party has already gained more first-vote, constituency seats than it is strictly speaking entitled to, based on its proportion of second-vote, list seats. If this occurs, then extra parliamentary seats, or additional mandates (*Überhangmandate*) are created, and the size of the *Bundestag* is increased accordingly.

It is easier to understand how the additional seats occur by looking at an example. If there are 100 parliamentary seats to be allocated to the *Bundestag* from one particular federal state, then half (50) are taken by the directly elected constituency candidates, via the first vote. The other 50 seats are allocated according to the parties' share of the second votes. Assuming that party A gained 40 per cent of the second votes, party B 35 per cent and party C 25 per cent, then the three parties would be allocated 40, 35 and 25 seats respectively, in line with the principle of proportional representation on the basis of the valid second/party votes cast.

Supposing, however, party A has gained 43 constituency seats via the first votes, i.e. three more than it is strictly speaking entitled to, on the basis of its share of the second vote. Suppose party B won only two constituencies and party C none. All the successful constituency candidates of any party are always permitted to retain those mandates. In this example party A would in fact be allocated not 40, but 43 seats, thus creating three additional, or extra mandates/seats. The final seat allocation for parties A, B and C would therefore be 43, 35 and 25 respectively, and the size of the parliament is increased from 100 to 103.

At *Land* elections 13 of the 16 federal states also permit additional mandates, if they occur. Only Bremen, Hamburg and the Saarland do not allow them. Although not many of these additional seats occurred in practice in the federal elections between 1949 and 1987 (the largest number was five in 1961), the number of instances increased in the new Germany. There were six extra mandates in 1990, 16 in 1994, 13 in 1998, and five in 2002. Between 1990 and 1998 the enlarged German territory contained 328 constituencies. That meant that 328 members of parliament were elected via the first votes and another 328 via the second votes, making a total of 656.

When the actual number of members of parliament increased to 672 in 1994 – as a result of the additional mandates – the German federal parliament certainly was one of the largest (and also one of the most expensive!) in the democratic world. For the federal election of 2002 the size of the *Bundestag* in Berlin was reduced to 598 – i.e. 299 deputies (*Abgeordnete*) chosen via the constituencies, with another 299 selected from the party lists. There were five additional mandates in 2002 – four for the SPD and one for the CDU, bringing the total number of members of the current *Bundestag* to 603. The four extra seats for the SPD were in Hamburg (see below), Thuringia and two in Saxony-Anhalt. The CDU gained one in Saxony.

An example of how such an extra mandate (*Überhangmandat*) actually occurred is the one gained by the SPD in Hamburg. According to the parties' share of the second vote, the twelve seats in the federal parliament in Berlin should have been allocated as follows: SPD five, CDU four, Greens two, FDP one.[1] However, when attention was turned to the first votes cast, it transpired that the SPD had won all six of the constituencies in Hamburg. Since the constituency candidates were entitled to retain the seats gained, the SPD was allocated not five, but six seats. In this way an extra mandate was created and the size of the new *Bundestag* was increased.

Because the German electoral system is fundamentally a proportional one, it is the voter's second vote that establishes the strength of the parties in parliament, and therefore decides who will become Federal Chancellor. A party which does not gain at least 5 per cent of the valid second votes does not normally gain any parliamentary seats. Consequently the second vote is actually more important (*wahlentscheidend*) than the first, even though, according to the results of electoral research questionnaires, quite a large proportion of German voters incorrectly think that the first vote is more important than the second. This is perhaps based on logically assuming that number one vote is more important than number two vote, even though this assumption is wrong. Other voters make the mistake of thinking that the two votes are of equal value. Such an assumption, although also incorrect, is possibly based on the fact that each vote elects an equal number of deputies.

Any German citizen over the age of 18 is eligible to vote, subject to residence requirements. Postal votes from German citizens living abroad are now admissible. If a German deputy dies or retires mid-term, he or she is simply replaced by the next person on the party list, so there are no by-elections, as in Great Britain, for example. An interesting feature of elections in Germany is that voters may, if they wish, 'split their ticket' (*Splitting*), by giving their first vote to a candidate from one party and their second vote to a different party. Research reveals that up to around 10 (maximum 15) per cent of voters cast their votes in this way at some federal elections.

The German Liberal Party (the Free Democrats) have often made a direct appeal during federal election campaigns for the second vote. The FDP, in particular, and the Greens too, have sometimes benefited in this way and entered parliament by clearing the 5 per cent hurdle via the second votes cast, even though nowadays they hardly ever win a constituency via the first votes. This can happen if a sufficient number of voters cast their first votes in favour of a candidate from either the CDU/CSU or the SPD but give their second votes to one of the smaller parties.

It is rare for candidates from parties other than the two main ones to win a constituency seat in the present political situation. In fact, another small party, the PDS (see above), has shown itself to be the exception to this rule at recent federal elections, since the party won the same four constituencies (three would have sufficed) in East Berlin in 1994 and 1998. In 2002 the PDS managed to win only two constituencies, again in east Berlin, perhaps partly due to constituency boundaries changes resulting from the reduction in the number of constituencies in Germany as a whole from 328 to 299. The new federal states in eastern Germany in general, and East Berlin in particular, are usually areas of strong electoral support for the PDS, often known as '*die ostdeutsche Volkspartei*' – the East German people's party, i.e. the party that represents the interests of voters in the east. Their overall support actually dwindled slightly at the 2002 federal election, although they still remained much stronger in the east than the west.

The phenomenon of splitting your two votes (*Splitting*) means that German voters have the option of voting for a coalition government if they so wish. This is of course made easier if the FDP or the Greens have issued a clear coalition statement before the election concerning which of the two big parties they intend to support after the election; this is usually, though not always, the case. Before the 2002 federal election it was clear that Alliance '90/the Greens wished to continue to offer their services as a coalition partner to the SPD after the election. The Liberals, however, deliberately made no coalition statement (*Koalitionsaussage*) and – in the view of some observers – suffered for it. They certainly did not do as well as they were hoping. According to one poll shortly before the 2002 election over half of those polled thought that the Liberals should have expressed a clear coalition preference, so that voters knew where the party stood.[2]

Splitting also means that discerning voters can use the two-vote system quite subtly, according to the electoral outcome they desire. At the 1998 federal election, for example, a number of PDS supporters in East Berlin gave their first vote to the PDS, because they wanted to ensure that their preferred party entered the *Bundestag* via the three-constituency rule. This appeared to some PDS supporters to be the safest option, since there was some doubt as to whether their party would clear the 5 per cent hurdle (1998: PDS 5.1 per cent). Some of those voters, unhappy with the performance of Kohl and the CDU/CSU, gave their second votes to the SPD, in order to bring about the change in power they wanted. It displayed a subtle approach and considerable refinement in voting behaviour.

2.3   A Three-party System Emerges

As a result of the tightening of the workings of the electoral system, in 1953 and 1956 the number of parties entering the *Bundestag* in Bonn was gradually reduced from 11 at the first federal election in 1949 to only three, following the 1961 federal elections. The three parties were the Social Democrats, the Christian Democrats, counting the CDU/CSU as one parliamentary party (*Fraktion*), since the conservative sister parties in fact form a joint parliamentary party after each election, and the Free Democrats. The FDP, the West German liberal party, had become the largest of the small parties, and the only remaining one, alongside the big two 'catch-all' or people's parties (*Volksparteien*), which cleared the 5 per cent clause at federal level in 1961.

The Free Democrats (FDP) had, by that time, managed to carve out a pivotal position for themselves in what had become a three-party system at federal level, adopting the role of third force (*die dritte Kraft*) in the (West) German party system. During the period of the 1957–61 government, the services of

Stimmzettel

für die Wahl zum Deutschen Bundestag im Wahlkreis 180
Wiesbaden
am 22. September 2002

Sie haben 2 Stimmen

hier 1 Stimme	hier 1 Stimme
für die Wahl	für die Wahl
eines / einer Wahlkreis-	einer Landesliste (Partei)
abgeordneten	- maßgebende Stimme für die Verteilung der Sitze insgesamt auf die einzelnen Parteien -
Erststimme	**Zweitstimme**

	Erststimme					Zweitstimme	
1	**Wieczorek-Zeul,** Heidemarie Lehrerin Wiesbaden Walkmühlstraße 39	**SPD**	Sozialdemokratische Partei Deutschlands	○	○	**SPD** — Sozialdemokratische Partei Deutschlands Hans Eichel, Heidemarie Wieczorek-Zeul, Klaus Wieshügel, Barbara Imhof, Erika Lotz	1
2	**Köhler,** Kristina Dipl.-Soziologin Wiesbaden Schönbergstraße 92	**CDU**	Christlich Demokratische Union Deutschlands	○	○	**CDU** — Christlich Demokratische Union Deutschlands Prof. Dr. Heinz Riesenhuber, Dr. Klaus W. Lippold, Erika Steinbach, Gerald Weiß, Bernd Siebert	2
3	**Janke,** Rudolf Dipl.-Volkswirt Wiesbaden Kleiststraße 7 A	**GRÜNE**	Bündnis 90/ DIE GRÜNEN	○	○	**GRÜNE** — Bündnis 90/DIE GRÜNEN Dr. Antje Vollmer, Joseph Fischer, Margareta Wolf, Matthias Berninger, Anna Lührmann	3
4	**Burghard,** Kai-Christofer Rechtsanwalt Wiesbaden Mittelweg 10	**FDP**	Freie Demokratische Partei	○	○	**FDP** — Freie Demokratische Partei Dr. Wolfgang Gerhardt, Dr. Hermann Otto Prinz zu Solms-Hohensolms-Lich, Dr. Heinrich Leonhard Kolb, Hans-Joachim Otto, Mechthild Dyckmans	4
					○	**REP** — DIE REPUBLIKANER Günter Haemer, Bert-Rüdiger Förster, Michael Langer, Ingeborg Godenau, Matthias Ottmar	5
6	**Möller,** Hans selbständig Bad Vilbel Oberurseler Straße 10	**PDS**	Partei des Demokratischen Sozialismus	○	○	**PDS** — Partei des Demokratischen Sozialismus Lukrezia Jochimsen, Pia Maier, Harry Siegert, Astrid Nord, Norbert Domes	6
					○	**Die Tier-schutz-partei** — Mensch Umwelt Tierschutz Jürgen Gerlach, Alfred Fischer, Hannelore Jansen, Margitta Marcian, Dieter Hamburger	7
					○	**NPD** — Nationaldemokratische Partei Deutschlands Doris Zutt, Volker Sachs, Stefan Rochow, Günter Seiffert, Steve Scheufler	8
					○	**GRAUE** — DIE GRAUEN - Graue Panther Karl Hüttinger, Wolfgang Dederichs, Iris Volk, Sibylle Schömig, Christa Klose	9
					○	**PBC** — Partei Bibeltreuer Christen Klaus-Peter Oberkinkhaus, Klaus Sydow, Wolfgang Schüler, Rudolf Schmidt, Leonore Müller	10
					○	**CM** — CHRISTLICHE MITTE - Für ein Deutschland nach GOTTES Geboten Josef Happel, Maria Stieh, Harald Hormel, Rita Kissling, Werner Biela	11
					○	**ödp** — Ökologisch-Demokratische Partei Jürgen Reuß, Martin Ratuschny, Eric Manneschmidt, Michael Seidling-Lewin, Christian Dörfler	12
13	**Hartmann,** Alexander Journalist Wiesbaden Köhlstraße 48	**BüSo**	Bürgerrechtsbewegung Solidarität	○	○	**BüSo** — Bürgerrechtsbewegung Solidarität Hartmut Cramer, Gabriele Liebig, Michael Weißbach, Louis Donath, Yousef Adam	13
					○	**Schill** — Partei Rechtsstaatlicher Offensive Frank Bücken, Hans-Günter Müller, Hubert Busch, Hermann Krauß, Eckhard Gathof	14

Figure 2.1   Ballot paper (2002)

the Free Democrats had not been required as a coalition partner, owing to one party (in this case the CDU/CSU) gaining an absolute majority (50.2 per cent). That was the only federal election from 1949 until the present day when this has occurred. From 1961 onwards the situation altered. Coalition government was the order of the day and so was the three-party system up until 1983.

The significance of coalition politics in the German political system was clear for all to see. The need to form coalition governments at federal level is often seen as the driving force behind the search for consensus rather than confrontation, and the role of the German electoral system has been commented on in this context by several German authors. These include for example Karl-Rudolf Korte, Wolfgang Rudzio, Dieter Nohlen, Emil Hübner and Dieter Roth, as well as a number of British and American authors, such as William E. Paterson, Gordon Smith, Geoffrey Roberts, Gerard Braunthal, Christian Söe and David P. Conradt. It is important to emphasise that the German electoral system is seen by many experts in the field as making an important contribution to the German polity overall.

During the period 1961–66 the FDP was again able to offer its services as a government coalition partner to the CDU/CSU. From 1966–69, partly as a reaction to the Federal Republic's first real economic crisis and the rise of the right-wing extremist NPD, the SPD and the CDU/CSU formed a Grand Coalition (*Große Koalition*) government, never to be repeated at federal level. From 1969 until 1982 the German liberal party transferred its allegiances from its established coalition partner, the Christian Democrats, to the Social Democrats, and became the junior coalition partner in four successive SPD/ FDP federal governments. The three-party system at federal level in Germany was by that time well established, and it continued until the Green Party cleared the 5 per cent hurdle for the first time at a federal election in 1983.

The time of the Grand Coalition (1966–69) was disastrous for the tiny FDP, with some 50 members of parliament sitting alone on the Opposition benches. The Federal Republic's electoral system, based on proportional representation with its 5 per cent cut-off clause, meant that between 1961 and 1983 a three-party system was firmly anchored in West Germany's political system: the dominant large parties, the CDU/CSU and the SPD, as well as the tiny FDP, were the only parties to enter the *Bundestag* in Bonn. Amazingly, 99 per cent of the second votes cast at the 1976 federal election were for those three parties.[3]

2.4   d'Hondt versus Niemeyer

From 1949 onwards the electoral system was of course based on PR and included a method of allocating seats in parliament devised by a Belgian Professor of Law and mathematician, Victor d'Hondt. This was called the highest average/number procedure (*Höchstzahlverfahren*). It involved dividing the number of votes cast for each party list in a federal election by one, two, three, and so on, and allocating the first seat to the party with the highest quotient, as in the example given in Table 2.1.

Table 2.1   d'Hondt method

11 seats to be allocated

	Party A	Party B	Party C
Votes	6000	4000	1800
divide by 1	6000 = 1st	4000 = 2nd	1800 = 6th
divide by 2	3000 = 3rd	2000 = 4th	900
divide by 3	2000 = 5th	1333 = 8th	600
divide by 4	1500 = 7th	1000 = 11th	450
divide by 5	1200 = 9th	800	360
divide by 6	1000 = 10th	666	300
Seats	6 seats	4 seats	1 seat

In 1985 a different method of seat allocation was adopted for federal elections. The new method was based upon a system devised by an English lawyer, Thomas Hare, and a German mathematician, Horst Niemeyer. There are different variations of this procedure, but essentially it slightly favours the small parties over the big ones. The Hare/Niemeyer method multiplies the number of second votes a party gains by the number of seats to be allocated, and then divides the result by the total number of the second (i.e. party) votes of all the parties that cleared the 5 per cent hurdle (see Table 2.2).

Had the Hare/Niemeyer method been in operation for the federal elections in 1976 and 1980, the FDP would have received one more seat in the *Bundestag* in each case, at the expense of the CDU. In 1983 the Greens would have been given one more seat in the federal parliament, again at the expense of the CDU. So the effect was minimal; it was, however, felt to be slightly unfair that cases arose – and this applied in some of the *Länder* too – where small parties such

Table 2.2   Hare/Niemeyer method

11 seats to be allocated

Total votes	Party A	Party B	Party C
11800	6000	4000	1800

$$\frac{\text{Total no. of seats} \times \text{party votes}}{\text{Total votes for all parties}}$$

5.59	3.73	1.68	
5 seats	3 seats	1 seats	
	+1	+1	
Seats awarded	5 seats	4 seats	2 seats

as the FDP or the Greens were being required to gain around 80,000 votes in order to win a seat in parliament, whilst the big parties were winning a seat with around 48,000 votes.[4]

2.5   Voter Turnout

Turnout at German elections in the Federal Republic has historically been amongst the highest in western democracies, although voting is not compulsory. Even at the first federal election in West Germany after the Second World War, when you might have expected the majority of the war-weary German electorate to have abstained, following their experiences between 1933 and 1945, there was nevertheless a 78.5 per cent turnout. That was the lowest figure at any West German federal election; indeed turnout, or electoral participation (*Wahlbeteiligung*) in Germany twice reached the staggering figure of over 90 per cent in the 1970s (see Table 2.3). These were record participation levels for a country where voting is not obligatory.

At the first all-German federal election of 1990 the turnout took a slight drop of course, given that the inhabitants of the former GDR had less experience of making a real choice in free elections. Turnout increased a little in 1994, although, predictably, the rates were slightly different in the old federal states in the west (80.2 per cent) and the new states in the east (73.6 per cent). By 1998 the overall turnout was back to over the 80 per cent mark again. Such high participation rates in a democratic system which does not have compulsory voting was explained to the author in an interview with the German expert on world electoral systems, Professor Dieter Nohlen, as follows: 'The German voter sees his right to vote as a duty to vote.'[5] This confirmed the oft-quoted German phrase that going out to vote is a priority for German citizens (*Wählen ist die erste Bürgerpflicht*).

Table 2.3 Turnout at federal elections

1949	78.5%	1953	85.8%	1957	87.8%	1961	87.7%
1965	86.8%	1969	86.7%	1972	91.1%	1976	90.7%
1980	88.6%	1983	89.1%	1987	84.3%	1990	77.8%
1994	79.0%	1998	82.3%	2002	79.1%		

Turnout tends to be slightly lower at regional (*Land*) elections. German voters clearly view a federal election as being a more important event than a regional one, and in any case a regional election is seen by some voters as an opportunity to give their politicians a warning, something to think about (*einen Denkzettel verpassen*). Those who choose to abstain (*Nichtwähler*) sometimes choose not to go to the polls at a *Landtagswahl* as a form of protest, whereas they are more likely to cast their vote at a *Bundestagswahl*, even if they are dissatisfied with the performance of their politicians. During a visit to the headquarters of the German electoral research institute, Forschungsgruppe Wahlen e.V. in Mannheim, the author was told that the German voter places elections in Germany in a clear order of priority: first, federal, next regional, then local, and finally European elections.[6]

When voter participation at recent federal elections is examined in terms of the old (western) federal states and the new (eastern) federal states, the turnout was higher in the west than the east. In 1994, for example, the overall turnout was 79 per cent: 82.2 per cent in the west, 73.6 per cent in the east. In 1998 the corresponding figures were 82.8 per cent in the west and 80.3 per cent in the east, with an overall turnout of 82.3 per cent. At the 2002 federal election the overall turnout of 79.1 per cent was broken down into 80.7 per cent in the west and 72.8 per cent in the east. Since German unity in 1990 participation in elections has been slightly lower in the eastern states, which is perhaps only to be expected, given the differing political cultures of the former GDR and FRG prior to 1990. Indeed, at the first all-German federal elections in 1990 the turnout dropped to 77.8 per cent, the lowest figure for a postwar federal election. However, as we have seen, the participation figure increased four years later and increased further in 1998.

Low turnout can of course affect the support for particular parties, and in some cases that can mean that smaller parties may fail to clear the 5 per cent hurdle. If, as a result, three rather than four parties enter parliament following a federal or regional election in Germany, the possible government coalition partners can be affected.

An example of this was seen in September 2001 following the elections to the Hamburg parliament (*Bürgerschaft*). The *Rechtsstaatlicher Offensive* party led by the controversial judge Ronald Schill (*'Richter Gnadenlos'*) would not have been able to join the new government coalition had the FDP not cleared the cut-off clause and agreed to join the CDU-led *Bürgerblock* coalition. This was the first regional government in the city state of Hamburg in 44 years which did not contain the SPD. Although all the emphasis at the time was on the new *Schillpartei*, which polled a staggering 19.4 per cent, the tiny FDP, which did not give a clear statement of support (*Koalitionsaussage*) for either the SPD or the CDU before the election, again played a key role. There was the usual *Zitterpartie* (nail-biting wait) to see if the Free Democrats would clear the 5 per cent hurdle. With a result of 5.1 per cent, it could hardly have been closer.

Similarly, the regional election in Berlin in October 2001 was influenced by the outstanding success of the party of democratic socialism (PDS), which gained nearly half of the vote (almost 48 per cent) in East Berlin. The PDS entered the regional parliament in Berlin (*Abgeordetenhaus*), as well as the SPD, the CDU, the Greens and the FDP, thus adding an extra dimension to the political situation. Owing to the allocation of mandates in the Berlin regional parliament, the federal government parties of SPD and the Greens needed the FDP to give them a majority. Although Schröder favoured that option, the failure of the Free Democrats to agree in the coalition negotiations – especially with regard to taxation – meant that a SPD/PDS regional government was formed in Berlin. The seat distribution and government coalition possibilities are obviously quite different if five rather than four, or four rather than three parties enter either the federal or a regional parliament. This underlines the importance of both the turnout and the cut-off clause in German elections.

At the April 2002 *Landtagswahl* in Sachsen-Anhalt, the last regional election to be held before the federal election, there was a low turnout, very low by German standards, of only 56 per cent. At the previous election four years earlier 70 per cent had turned out to vote. Several factors played a part in the results. In general terms, however, it must be said that German voters in the new federal states have a different political culture, which often affects their electoral behaviour.

In the regional election in question, in the federal state of Saxony-Anhalt, the PDS again revealed itself to be a major political force, even nudging ahead of the SPD, although on this occasion it was the CDU, the other main player in the East German three-party system, which gained the most votes. The FDP surprised many observers, including its own supporters, by winning over 13 per cent of the vote, despite having performed very badly in polls in the new federal states in the years preceding that result. The Greens, extremely weak in the east, failed to enter the *Landtag* in Magdeburg, as predicted. This time there was no strong electoral presence on the extreme Right of the political spectrum; the German People's Party (DVU), which gained almost 13 per cent of the vote in 1998, did not contest the 2002 regional election. Although Ronald Schill's party, *Rechtsstaatlicher Offensive*, did contest the election, the party gained just under 5 per cent of the vote and was thus prevented from taking up parliamentary representation.

2.6 Influence of the Electoral System on the Development of the Party System

The electoral system and its 5 per cent clause have, over the years, exerted considerable influence on both individual parties and the party system in general at both federal and regional level in German politics. Certainly, if voter turnout is a reliable indicator, it would appear that generally speaking a high proportion of German voters perceive the German federal electoral system as encouraging them to go out and vote. As they are able to cast two votes in a system based on PR, there would seem to be few concerns about 'wasted votes'. In fact even if a German voter casts just one of the two votes, it is still valid. The voter does not have to register both votes, although in practice most do precisely that.

The fundamental decision to adopt a system based on PR, rather than a majority one, meant that more scope was given to the smaller parties. Indeed, it is true to say that the survival of the FDP at federal level over many years was inextricably linked to the specific provisions of German electoral law. Coalition governments were encouraged and a two-party system, such as the one in Britain or the USA, was usually avoided. The fact that the large parties also gained just representation in line with their electoral support – the SPD had been seriously disadvantaged in past German political systems (see 1.2) – was a positive influence.

In the early post-war years in West Germany the tightening of the application of the cut-off clause had the effect of reducing the number of parties entering parliament at federal level. As we have seen, the electoral system promoted the development of a three-party system between 1961 and 1983. It nevertheless proved flexible enough to embrace a four-party system, with the arrival of the Green Party in federal politics in 1983, following a long succession of achievements at local and regional level. From 1990 onwards, up until 2002, it became a five-party system, with the advent of the PDS.

In terms of party concentration, the percentage of the West German electorate who voted for the two main people's parties at federal elections between 1949 and the mid-1970s increased steadily from just over 60 per cent to over 90 per cent in both 1972 and 1976. This meant of course that the percentage of those supporting any parties other than the CDU/CSU or the SPD decreased correspondingly from nearly 40 per cent in 1949 to just below 9 per cent in 1976.[7]

Gordon Smith, in his seminal text *Democracy in Western Germany*,[8] wrote at the time of five stages of development in the (West) German party system between 1945 and the mid-1970s. Although, as the author states, these developments did not always contain sharp lines of demarcation, the five stages serve as a useful guide to the first three decades of the Federal Republic. Stage one 1945–49 was one of nascence, and stage two 1949–53 was one of diffusion. Stage three 1953–66 was one of imbalance, whilst stage four 1966–69 (Grand Coalition) was one of transition. Gordon Smith described the final stage, at the time of writing in 1978/79, from 1969 onwards, as one of balance. Throughout these different stages of development the electoral system continued to play a key role in the party system.

Having emerged initially as a multi-party system and having gradually developed by 1961 into a three-party system (referred to by some authors as a 'two-and-a-half party system', acknowledging the special position of the tiny FDP). When the Greens were able to satisfy the stipulations of electoral law at federal level in 1983, it developed into a four-party system. Following the new developments in German politics since 1989/90, the electoral system proved to be flexible enough to cope with what became a five-party system.

On 2 December 1990, for the first all-German elections, the German polity managed to incorporate the party representing East German interests, the PDS, by implementing two separate 5 per cent clauses for the old and new federal states. And then, by means of the three-constituency rule, provided for the PDS (with over a fifth of the vote in the east) to gain parliamentary representation four years later.

2.7 Continuity and Change in the Party System

Whilst the present party system in Germany differs from that of previous decades, the changes have been accompanied by a strong element of continuity. This has been clearly linked to the underlying presence and contribution of the electoral system. Changes and developments in the method of voting have, as we have already seen, exercised a significant influence on individual parties and party systems at both federal and *Land* level. Yet at the same time the electoral system has, ever since the postwar period, performed as a sort of anchor man, providing stability and balance against the background of proportionality in German politics.

Following the first federal election in 1949 the two big people's parties, the CDU/CSU and the SPD emerged neck-and-neck, with 31.0 and 29.2 per cent of the vote respectively, although in the first parliamentary vote – in the converted teacher training college used as the *Bundestag* in the provisional capital, *Bonn am Rhein* – Konrad Adenauer was elected Federal Chancellor on the strength of just one vote (his own). A CDU/CSU-FDP-DP government took office. Important changes in the electoral system in 1953 (see 1.6.1) meant that the number of parties entering the federal parliament was reduced from eleven to six. There were also three independent members of parliament, not attached to any political party.[9] The number of members of the *Bundestag* in 1953 increased from 402 to 487. A fourth party, the GB/BHE (the Refugees' Party), joined the federal government from 1953 to 1955.

Following the electoral law of 1956 and the 1957 federal elections, after the FDP had left Adenauer's coalition government in 1956, a CDU/CSU/DP government ruled, without the Free Democrats, from 1957 to 1961. The concentration of the party system was continuing, as this time only four parties cleared the 5 per cent hurdle, resulting from Adenauer's support of the tiny *Deutsche Partei*. This was really only a minor change amidst the continuity of developments in the party system, which by 1961 had become firmly established as a three-party system, also known as a 'two-and-a-half party system,' (see above) – a reference to the FDP. In terms of size, membership and electoral support, the Liberals were certainly no more than a 'half' compared to the two major parties, yet in terms of political influence and government participation they could be regarded as a 'full' party. The German electoral system has played a major part in affecting the role and functions of the FDP in the party system.

Notes

1   Information taken from Bundestagswahl (2002), *Eine Analyse der Wahl vom 22*, Nr 108, September, Mannheim: Berichte der Forschungsgruppe Wahlen e.V., p. 82.

2   This was explained to the author during a seminar at the headquarters of the German polling institute infratest dimap in Berlin on 20 September 2002, as part of an ASGP election visit, supported by the DAAD, from 18–23 September, to observe and report on the 2002 federal election.

3   Korte, Karl-Rudolf (1998) *Wahlen in der BRD*, Bonn: Bundeszentrale für politische Bildung, p. 105.

4   For example there was a court ruling in Bavaria in 1992 which resulted in the adoption of the Hare/Niemeyer method for Bavarian elections. This was after the opposition parties, taking up the initiative of the Bavarian FDP, pointed out that at the Bavarian state elections on 14 October 1990 the CSU needed only 47,980 votes in order to gain a mandate in the Munich parliament, whereas the FDP required 81,905. This figure is arrived at by dividing the total number of votes gained by a party by the number of parliamentary seats it gains. If the Hare/Niemeyer method of seat allocation had actually been applied to that election, the CSU would have forfeited six mandates and the Bavarian SPD one. See Peter James (1995), 'The Free State of Bavaria: A Special Case', *Representation*, Vol. 33, No. 1, Spring/Summer.

5   'Der Deutsche sieht das nicht nur als Wahlrecht sondern auch als Wahlpflicht', interview with Prof. Dr Dieter Nohlen at the Institute für Politik in Heidelberg 15 May 2001.

6   Bundestagswahl, Landtagswahl, Kommunalwahl, Europawahl. Interview with Dr Dieter Roth, Head of the Forschungsgruppe Wahlen electoral research institute in Mannheim 14 May 2001.

7   Korte, op. cit., p. 102.

8   Gordon Smith (1979), *Democracy in Western Germany. Parties and Politics in the Federal Republic*, London: Heinemann, p. 102.

9   Geoffrey K. Roberts (2000), *German Politics Today*, Manchester and New York: Manchester University Press, p. 55.

Chapter 3

Protest and Disaffection: The Electoral System is Put to the Test

3.1 Extra-Parliamentary Opposition – A Change in the Voting System?

In the 1960s, following the celebrated West German economic miracle (*Wirtschaftswunder*) of the previous decade and the gradual dominance of the political system by Adenauer and the Christian Democrats, the party system had become more concentrated and firmly established. When only the two main *Volksparteien* and the liberal Free Democrats, by then in danger of being seen as a mere appendage to the CDU/CSU, entered the federal parliament in Bonn in 1961, the party system was starting to look frozen, if not stale. Very few female representatives took up places in the Bundestag, which was dominated by middle-aged men in white shirts and dark suits.

In the run-up to the 1961 federal election it had been felt strongly in some circles that it was time for Konrad Adenauer, who by that time was 85 years old, to step down as Chancellor. Agreements amongst several parties had apparently been reached and the FDP had fought the 1961 election campaign on the basis of forming a coalition government with the CDU/CSU, but *without* Adenauer.

In fact, Adenauer stubbornly refused to stand down until half way through the period of legislature in 1963; so in the event Adenauer was re-elected as Chancellor in 1961 and the FDP gained the reputation of having gone back on its word (*Umfallpartei*), although they claimed they had been let down by others. Furthermore, with the building of the Berlin Wall on 13 August 1961, and Adenauer's reaction to it, (the federal election took place in mid-September), serious developments in the political situation were starting to take place.

As the Federal Republic began to suffer its first economic problems, a new right-wing extremist party, the NPD (*Nationaldemokratische Partei Deutschlands*) was founded in November 1964. The rapid rise in support for this protest party presented a new problem for West Germany's established democratic parties, as the NPD began to gain a series of regional successes, clearing the 5 per cent clause in several *Land* parliaments between 1966 and 1969.

For example, in the regional elections to the Bavarian *Landtag* on 20 November 1966 the NPD replaced the FDP by clearing the 10 per cent hurdle; Bavaria was the only federal state to have a 10 per cent hurdle in regional elections. It was changed to 5 per cent in 1973, bringing it into line with all the other western states. The NPD added insult to injury by ousting the Liberals in their former Bavarian stronghold of Central Franconia (*Mittelfranken*). In April 1968 the neo-nazi NPD gained very nearly ten (9.8) per cent of the vote in the regional elections in Baden-Württemberg. This, along with the other NPD successes, was viewed at the time with great concern by those wishing to protect and preserve West Germany's fledgling democracy.

The difficult political circumstances of the Grand Coalition government between 1966 and 1969 were aggravated by the whole Extra-Parliamentary Opposition movement (APO – *Außerparlamentarische Opposition*). This was a protest movement, very strong around that time, which consisted mainly of students and young people who wished to demonstrate against what they saw as the stalemate political situation in general, as well as the emergency laws (*Notstandsgesetze*) of 1968 and the concentration of the German press in particular. APO was also influenced very considerably by the American protest movement against the war in Vietnam. In Germany it saw itself as offering a sort of counter-balance to make up for the lack of an effective Opposition in the federal parliament at the time.

As a result of the NPD successes, those who wanted to avoid having a party of the extreme Right represented in the *Bundestag*, and the tarnished image of West Germany abroad they feared would accompany it, were faced with three alternatives. Firstly, they could apply to the Federal Constitutional Court in Karlsruhe to have the NPD banned. However time was getting short with the date of the federal election (28 September 1969) fast approaching, and the attempt to have the SRP and the KPD banned in the 1950s had been extremely time-consuming. In any case, there was no certainty that a ban would be forthcoming.

The second possibility was to consider trying to amend the electoral law's cut-off clause from a 5 per cent to a 10 per cent hurdle, as it was assumed that the NPD would be unlikely to gain 10 per cent of the second votes at federal level. At the time, however, 5 per cent was beginning to look more and more likely. Again time was short.

The third alternative was simply to do nothing and trust in 'the common sense', as some observers saw it, of the electorate. This was in fact the approach taken. Eleven *Land* elections were held between 1966 and 1969 in West Germany; the NPD entered seven regional parliaments as a result, yet at the 1969 federal election the party gained 'only' 4.3 per cent (1.4 million votes).[1] Consequently the new neo-nazi party failed to gain parliamentary representation at federal level in Bonn. Opponents of the NPD, who had been extremely apprehensive about the kind of image a *Bundestag* in Bonn containing a right-wing extremist party would present to foreign observers, breathed a huge sigh of relief.

3.2 Proposed Changes in the Electoral Law

During the coalition negotiations between the CDU/CSU and the SPD in 1966 there had been serious discussion of the question of electoral reform. This was encouraged by research data that suggested that it would be in the interests of the CDU, and possibly the SPD too, to adopt a majority voting system. It even got as far as specific proposals being put before a commission. The FDP protested violently of course, claiming that the big 'catch-all' parties just wanted to get rid of the small parties completely. They spoke of the end of freedom (*Ende der Freiheit*). It was only when new SPD research revealed that a majority system would probably *not* serve its best interests that enthusiasm for electoral reform waned.

Until 1969 some had thought that a proportional voting system was perhaps incapable of producing a real change of power at federal level. That theory was proved wrong with the advent of a new social-liberal coalition government in 1969. Even though the FDP polled its worst result ever at a federal election (5.8 per cent), the existing electoral system again proved workable in practice (*arbeitsfähig*). The effect of the 5 per cent hurdle was clear for all to see: a party with 4.3 per cent of the vote was not represented in the *Bundestag*, whilst one with 5.8 per cent was. The party in question, the FDP, was not only represented but was also able to participate in bringing about the Federal Republic's first real change in power. It did that by offering its services as a government coalition partner to the Social Democrats, for the first time at federal level, although the Christian Democrats were in fact still the largest party in parliament in 1969.

The only other serious proposals for electoral reform in post-war Germany had been put forward by Konrad Adenauer in 1956 at a time when he was losing patience with the Free Democrats generally, and was angered in particular by the FDP opposition to his plans to give up the Saarland, which had been placed under French administration in 1945. In the event the Saarland joined the Federal Republic in 1957, after a plebiscite. Adenauer threatened to introduce a so-called *Grabenwahlsystem*. This would have created a *Graben* (trench) between the two-vote systems, which operated for the 1953 federal election.

Such a system would have affected the FDP badly and, it was thought at the time, have advantaged the Christian Democrats by placing greater emphasis on the constituency vote, and therefore veering towards a system of majority voting (*Mehrheitswahlrecht*). The proposal was dropped when the Liberals fought back by changing from the CDU to the SPD as government coalition partner in North Rhine Westphalia, West Germany's largest federal state. This was intended as a warning to Adenauer as to what might be possible in Bonn. As the so-called *Grabenwahlsystem* was abandoned, one SPD parliamentarian commentated in a joke at the expense of Adenauer and the CDU that anyone who digs a trench (*Graben*) falls in it himself.

3.3   The Emergence of *Politikverdrossenheit* (Disillusionment with Politics)

The new SPD/FDP federal government, with its slender twelve-seat majority in Bonn, survived for just over three years of what should have been a four-year period of legislature. Chancellor Brandt's bold, but in some circles controversial, *Ostpolitik* policy had caused some members of both government parties to transfer their loyalties to the Opposition. This precipitated the first of only two instances so far of an attempt to remove a sitting Federal Chancellor by means of a constructive vote of no confidence, invoking article 67 of the constitution. The attempt in April 1972 to oust Willy Brandt and replace him with the CDU/CSU candidate Rainer Barzel failed by two votes.

After a new, premature federal election was held in November 1972 (federal elections were not due until 1973), at which the SPD became the largest party (by a whisker) in the *Bundestag* for the first time, it seemed as if a critical phase in West German politics was over. That conclusion could certainly have been drawn from the electoral turnout (*Wahlbeteiligung*), which in 1972 was the highest ever, surpassing 91 per cent. At the following federal election four years later turnout was again over 90 per cent. These were truly amazing figures for a country where voting was not compulsory!

However, in 1982 a second vote of no confidence in an SPD Chancellor – this time it was Helmut Schmidt leading a social-liberal coalition in Bonn

– was attempted. On that occasion it succeeded. Helmut Kohl became Federal Chancellor as a result of a successful parliamentary vote of no confidence in October 1982. The second major change in power in the history of the Federal Republic was controversial at the time, since it was not confirmed by the German voters until another premature election was held in March 1983.

At the end of the 1980s the German term *Politikverdrossenheit* (disillusionment or disaffection with politics)[2] appeared. It coincided with a time when a right-wing extremist party, *die Republikaner* (the Republicans), was achieving some success in both the 1989 European and German regional elections (especially in West Berlin). Voter apathy set in and there was a general decline in electoral turnout, following the very high, record figures of the mid-seventies (see above). A number of financial and other scandals involving politicians and parties – two of the most infamous ones were the Flick Affair and the Barschel Affair in the 1990s – led to a general disillusionment with both the political system and politicians. The situation was not helped at a time when parliamentarians were voting themselves big pay rises whilst asking the voters to tighten their belts at times of economic stringency.

In 1992/93 the German Federal President, Richard von Weizsäcker, supported those who took the view that the state had gone stale (*Staatsverdrossenheit*), and the parties too (*Parteienverdrossenheit*). Some sections of the German population were convinced that their politicians and parties were carving up the system according to their own vested interests, and many German voters experienced a feeling of apathy towards the political process in general, and the electoral process in particular.[3]

Notes

1   Gerard Braunthal (1996), *Parties and Politics in Modern Germany*, Westview, pp. 104–105.
2   For a fuller definition of the term see Charlie Jeffery and Ruth Whittle (eds) (1997), *Germany Today*, Arnold, pp. 153–154.
3   See Gerard Braunthal (1996), *Parties and Politics in Modern Germany*, Westview Press, p. 2.

Chapter 4

Regional and Local Electoral Systems: Party Finance

4.1 Regional Elections

Although all the German federal states operate a proportional electoral system for choosing a new state parliament (*Landtagswahlen*), there is some variation in detail. Seven of Germany's 16 federal states apply the d'Hondt method of PR allocation. The remaining nine use the Hare/Niemeyer method (see 2.3). The size of the state parliament, and even the name by which it is known, will of course vary, according to the size of the particular state. Whilst 13 of the 16 regional parliaments are known as the *Landtag*, for example *der sächsische Landtag* (with 120 seats) in Dresden, or *der bayerische Landtag* (with 180 seats) in Munich, in Berlin the regional parliament is known as the *Abgeordnetenhaus* (with 150 seats), in Bremen the *Bürgerschaft* has 100 seats, and the Hamburg *Bürgerschaft* has 121 seats.

Half of the *Länder* now elect their regional parliaments every four years and the other half hold elections every five years, in order to avoid the sort of 'bunching' of elections that occurred initially in the new united Germany. In 1994, the so-called *Superwahljahr*, 19 elections, including those at federal and European level, took place over ten months. A repetition of that situation was avoided by the time of the 1998 national poll, with the period of legislature in some federal states having been increased from four to five years, and in 2002 there was only one *Landtagswahl*, in Sachsen-Anhalt in April, in the run-up to the *Bundestagswahl* in September. In 2003 only four regional contests were planned for February (Lower Saxony and Hesse), May (Bremen) and September (Bavaria).

In the early years of the Federal Republic Bavaria was the *only* federal state to have a two-vote system for *Land* elections; nowadays ten of the 16 *Länder* give their voters two votes at a regional election, with Baden-Württemberg, Bremen, Hamburg, North-Rhine Westphalia, Saarland and Schleswig-Holstein operating a one-vote system. Whilst some states divide the number of constituency and party list seats equally, for example, Saxony with 60/60, Thuringia with 44/44, or Hesse with 55/55, others have an unequal split, for example Schleswig-Holstein with 45/30, Lower Saxony with 100/55, or Berlin with 90/60.[1]

Even federal states where the voter has only one vote in a regional election, like Baden-Württemberg, whose regional parliament contains 120 seats, operate with both constituencies (70) and list seats (50). This involves a dual interpretation of the voter's wishes, as expressed by his or her single vote. This makes the voting system operated for regional elections in Baden-Württtenberg the most complicated one of the 16.

The vast majority of states operate a closed/fixed list system (*starre Listen*), which means that, just as in federal elections, the order of the candidates on the party lists cannot be altered by the voter. The federal state of Bavaria, however, is an exception to this rule: it is more flexible with its more open list of candidates (*lose, gebundene Listen*), allowing the Bavarian voters to cast their vote for a specific candidate on the party list if they wish to do so. As we have seen, Baden-Württemberg offers its voters constituency candidates only, even though the candidates' parties derive some recognition from the way in which the votes are cast.

All 16 of the German states have a 5 per cent cut-off clause at regional level. Bavaria had a 10 per cent clause until 1973. Under that system a party had to gain at least 10 per cent of the valid second votes cast in any one of Bavaria's seven regional government districts (*Regierungsbezirke*). In Berlin, Brandenburg and Schleswig-Holstein the alternative to gaining at least 5 per cent is gaining at least one direct mandate. In Saxony the alternative is two direct seats.

However it should also be remembered that in Bremen the 5 per cent clause is applied separately to Bremen and Bremerhaven. In Brandenburg it does not apply to the Sorb minority, and in Schleswig-Holstein the cut-off clause is not applied to the tiny SSW (*Südschleswigsche Wählerverein*) minority party.

Only three *Länder* (Bremen, Hamburg and Saarland) do not permit *Überhangmandate* (additional mandates – see 2.1). In these three states the voter has only one vote and the parliamentary mandates are allocated from party lists only, with no constituency seats. The other states, which do allow the recognition of additional mandates, usually balance out (*Ausgleich*) the seats created via compensation seats, rather than increasing the number of seats in the regional parliament, which is what happens at federal level. Turnout at regional elections in West Germany during the 1970s was very high – around 80 per cent, but it has decreased since unification – closer to an average of around 65–70 per cent now. Electoral participation tends to be lower in the eastern states than in the west.

It is seen as very important that the guiding principle of proportional representation in the voting systems of the various federal states is maintained, since the interests of their citizens are represented in the second chamber, the *Bundesrat*, according to the population size of each *Land*. Because the results of regional elections can change the colour of the *Land* governments, it sometimes happens that the majorities obtaining in the lower chamber (*Bundestag*) and the upper chamber (*Bundesrat*) are different.

That was certainly the case under part of Helmut Schmidt's social-liberal coalition (1974–82). In 1997, in the final year of the CDU/CSU/FDP federal coalition, the SPD had an absolute majority in three federal states, whilst that was the case for the CDU only in Saxony and the CSU in Bavaria. Helmut Kohl's conservative-liberal coalition government held power in the *Bundestag*, the lower house of parliament, whilst the SPD, in opposition, simultaneously had a majority in the *Bundesrat*, the upper house.

The situation following the 2002 federal election was just the other way round: the red/green government was returned to power on 22 September 2002, with a nine-seat majority in the first chamber (*Bundestag*) but no majority at all in the second chamber (*Bundesrat*), which was controlled by the parties of the Opposition.

4.2 Local Elections

Wolfgang Rudzio, in his standard text on Germany's political system, refers to the three tiers of devolution of power (*drei Ebenen mit jeweiligen Volksvertretungen*) [2] when referring to the way in which the German state is organised. He adds, however, that even though article 28 of the constitution (Art. 28 (2) GG) states that municipalities, or communes, (*Gemeinden*) must have the right to regulate their own affairs within the limits set by the law ('das Recht, alle Angelegenheiten der örtlichen Gemeinschaft im Rahmen der Gesetze in eigener Verantwortung zu regeln'), the vertical separation of powers in the decentralised federal framework often bears more resemblance in practice to a two-tier (*Bund/Länder*) system. This is because it is the federation and the federal states that jointly decide what sources of finance are available to the municipalities at local level.

Nevertheless, at local level (*auf kommunaler Ebene*) German citizens must have the right to elect the people who will represent them on their parish, town and district councils (*Gemeinderäte*, *Stadträte* and *Kreistage*). Even the *Gemeinde*, or commune, i.e. the smallest administrative unit in the German

Table 4.1   Electoral systems used for *Land* elections

Land	Period	Seats	No. of votes	Balance*	Dir./Lis	Allocation	Cut-off
Ba.Wü.	4 yrs	120	1	Yes	70/50	d'H #	5%
Bav.	4 yrs	180	2	Yes	H/N #	5%	5%
Berlin	4 yrs	150	2	Yes	90/60	H/N	5% (1)
Brand.	5 yrs	88	2	Yes	44/44	H/N	5% (1)
Brem.	4 yrs	100	1	None*	List**	D/H	5%
Hamb.	4 yrs	121	1	None*	List**	D/H	5%
Hesse	4 yrs	110	2	Yes	55/55	H/N	5%
Me-Po	4 yrs	71	2	Yes	36/35	H/N	5%
N-Sa.	5 yrs	155	2	Yes	100/55	D/H	5%
NRW	5 yrs	201	1	Yes	151/50	H/N	5%
Rh.Pf	5 yrs	105	2	Yes	51/50	H/N	5%
Saarl.	5 yrs	51	1	None	List**	D/H	5%
Sachs.	5 yrs	120	2	Yes	60/60	D/H	5% (2)
Sa An	4 yrs	99	2	Yes	49/50	H/N	5%
S-H	4 yrs	75	1	Yes	45/30	D/H	5% (1)
Thur.	5 yrs	88	2	Yes	44/44	H/N	5%

Notes

*   Whether or not additional mandates (*Überhangmandate*), should they occur, are 'balanced out' by not increasing the size of the regional parliament. Bremen, Hamburg and the Saarland do not permit additional mandates.

**   In Bremen, Hamburg and the Saarland only party list seats are allocated – there are no constituency seats at regional elections. Bremen has 80 seats and Bremerhaven 20.

\#   The Hare/Niemeyer method of allocating seats favours the small parties very slightly over the d'Hondt highest average method (see 2.3).

Source: adapted from information from various sources, including Korte (1998).

system, elects people to represent it. Since 1 January 1996 people who hold the nationality of any member state of the EU have both active and passive voting rights in local and European elections in Germany. The Maastricht Treaty stipulated that you do not have to possess German nationality in order to vote or stand for election in local elections.

There is considerable variety and complexity to be found in the way in which the different federal states elect their representatives locally. Such procedures may be the equivalent of selecting a village or town council. Several small administrative units, or communes, often form a *Landkreis*, and larger towns form a joint *Stadtkreis*. An increasing number of states in recent years have reduced the voting age for local elections from eighteen to sixteen. The first example of this was in Lower Saxony and Schleswig-Holstein in 1996. Other *Länder* have since followed suit. Polling at local level normally takes place at either four or five-year intervals, except in Bavaria, where it is every six years.

Whilst some form of PR, though not always personalised PR, is usually used at local level, the details can vary. The Saarland and Hesse, for instance, use closed lists, whilst Saxony, Mecklenburg-West Pomerania, Lower Saxony and others use free/open lists. In the Rhineland-Palatinate, Baden-Württemberg and Bavaria, each voter at a local election has as many votes as there are members of the local council to elect. The last two of these federal states both permit the use of two unusual electoral devices.

The first of these devices – *kumulieren* – permits the voter, if he or she wishes, to cast, or 'accumulate' up to three votes for one particular candidate on a party list. In this way strong preferences for individual politicians can be expressed within the party list, and often is. The second somewhat unusual electoral device – *panaschieren* – allows the Baden-Württemberg and Bavarian voters in local elections to give their votes to candidates on different party lists, should they wish to support representatives from various political groupings. The use of these two devices (*kumulieren* and *panaschieren*) is optional. Analyses of electoral behaviour in various reports by the *Forschungsgruppe Wahlen* Research Institute in Mannheim show that many voters (though by no means all) do avail themselves of this opportunity[3] at local elections in Germany's two most southern states.

Although the parties contesting local elections are also governed by German party law (*das Parteiengesetz*), at local level groups of voters are permitted to join together and form a communal voters' association (*Freie Wählergemeinschaft*). There have been recent developments to encourage such voter associations at federal level. The different types of constitution adopted for regulating local politics in the different German regions, such as the *Norddeutsche Ratsverfassung*, the *Magistratsverfassung*, the *Bürgermeisterverfassung* and the *Süddeutsche Verfassung* mean that the way in which the election of local officials and mayors functions sometimes varies considerably. For example mayors and lord mayors are elected for eight years in Baden-Württemberg, for six years in Bavaria and Hessen, for five years in North-Rhine Westphalia, and in the Rhineland Palatinate part-time, honorary mayors serve for five years but full-time mayors and lord mayors for ten.

At local polls in Hessen, the Saarland and NRW each voter has only one vote. In five of the federal states the voter has up to three votes each, in Bavaria and Baden-Württemberg the voter has as many votes available as there are representatives to be elected. In Thuringia and Schleswig-Holstein each voter has as many votes as there are constituency candidates to be selected.

According to some of the German polling research institutes German voters rate participation in local elections as more important than European elections, since in a local poll they have the opportunity of choosing their local representatives for their own particular area.[4] This is, understandably, viewed by many citizens as being more relevant to their everyday lives than a European poll, grand as it might sound.

Voters in local elections are less willing to forgive and forget the shortcomings of their elected representatives than is the case at a federal poll. That means that the outcome of local elections in Germany is often unpredictable.

4.3 Party Finance

In recent years the question of financing political parties and elections has moved centre-stage. This is not only due to the spiraling costs of election campaigns but also as a result of recent financial scandals involving both the main parties. Above all the revelation towards the end of 1999 that the Christian Democrats in general and former Chancellor Helmut Kohl in particular had set up secret bank accounts to help finance party campaigns (*Schwarzgeldaffäre*) put the whole issue of party finance in a new context. Another scandal, on a much smaller scale, with the SPD in the state of NRW in 2001 again focussed the spotlight on matters of party finance.

These two most recent scandals brought back memories of the infamous Flick Affair of 1983, when the three main German political parties all used front organisations as a means of avoiding the payment of tax on party donations.

Voter apathy and disillusionment with both politicians and politics in general (*Politikverdrossenheit*) set in, as the scandal affected the highest level of political power, including the resignation of the federal economics minister at the time, Graf Otto Lambsdorff of the FDP.

With reference to party finance, there are fundamentally two main sources of funding for political parties in Germany today – private and state finance. Private finance comes from four areas. Firstly, money accruing from party membership fees (unlike Great Britain, there is a sliding scale of membership fee according to income); secondly, party donations; thirdly, income from party funds; fourthly, miscellaneous income.

State finance covers three areas. Firstly, annual subsidies based on the number of votes a party gained at European, federal and regional elections, amounting to just under one euro per vote, once a party has achieved over 0.5 per cent of the valid second votes; secondly, annual subsidies for the parties' donations and contributions, and thirdly, tax breaks for private contributors and donors.

In terms of membership contributions, the SPD, with its greater number of members, has always outdone the other parties. In 1999 the SPD amassed over €80 million in membership fees, compared with almost €54 million for the CDU, just over €10 million for the CSU, 10.7 million for the Greens, €5.5 million for the FDP, and €9 million for the PDS. The Social Democrats were the only German party to gain over half of its finances from membership fees.

The biggest gainers from donations (*Spenden*) were the CDU, who derived around a quarter of its election expenses from this source. Funds donated to the CDU were nearly double those donated to the SPD. The Free Democrats usually gain the least money from membership dues, but they do better than the other parties – with the exception of the two major parties – on donations, which in 1999 accounted for approximately 40 per cent of their finances.

In 1999 the membership of the SPD, 755,966, brought in €80.5 million, whilst the CDU membership of 638,056 amounted to €53.9 million. As the FDP is a low membership party, the €5.5 million it raised from members of the party was less than a fifth of its total income. Figures published for the main German parties in 1999 revealed the following totals sums in millions of euros: SPD – 156.5, CDU – 132.4, CSU – 32.6, Greens – 26.3, FDP- 23.6, PDS – 20.8.[5] These figures included amounts from four sources: membership contributions, donations from firms and private individuals, payments from the state to reimburse election expenses linked to votes gained at the previous election, and miscellaneous items.

A separate issue is that of election costs incurred by issuing polling cards, expenses for election officials etc. Such costs escalated from the equivalent of €2.4 million for the federal election in 1953 to a massive €58.4 million in 1998. These sums included all the costs involved in the running of the election in the different federal states and all their electoral districts.[6]

Notes

1   All figures from Korte, *Wahlen in der Bundesrepublik Deutschland*, p. 72.
2   Wolfgang Rudzio (2001), *Das politische System der Bundesrepublik Deutschland*, Hagen: Polis, p. 266.
3   This fact was confirmed to the author in an interview with Dieter Roth, the Head of *Forschungsgruppe Wahlen* in Mannheim on 14 May 2001.
4   According to an infas poll in 1991, quoted on p. 79 of Korte (1998), 62 per cent of voters questioned rated voting in a federal election as 'very important' (*sehr wichtig*). The respective figures for regional, local and European elections were 34, 28, and 15.
5   Information taken from *Globus Infografik* Ab-7614, 4 March 2002.
6   Figures taken from *Globus Infografik* Ab-7799, 3 June 2002.

Chapter 5

The Developing Pattern of Federal Elections

From 1949 until the present day a clear pattern of development in German federal elections (*Bundestagswahlen*) has emerged. In general terms, this can be divided into approximately nine phases. The 2002 election will be treated separately, since it was a unique event.

5.1 Phase One

In the initial phase of the nascent party system it seemed as if a multi-party system, in the Weimar mould, would emerge. As has already been demonstrated, the fact that this did not happen is due in no small measure to the nature of the new electoral system that was introduced. The specific way in which the 5 per cent clause was tightened (see 1.6.1ff.) was in fact instrumental in assisting the reduction of the number of parties that entered the national parliament.

At the very first federal election in August 1949 the two main parties in West Germany, the Social Democrats and the Christian Democrats, emerged neck-and-neck, with the CDU leader, Konrad Adenauer, being confirmed in the parliamentary vote one month later, on 15 September 1949 in the *Bundestag* in Bonn as the first Federal Chancellor, on the strength of his own vote. Despite the closeness of the election result (CDU/CSU 31 per cent versus SPD 29.2 per cent), giving the CDU/CSU a mere eight seat majority, Adenauer was able to form a government coalition consisting of CDU/CSU, FDP and DP.

The new government at once began to establish itself and stamp its authority on the emerging party system, even though some ten parties plus independents sat in the *Bundestag*. Due partly to the promotion of the social market economy at a time when the main opposition party, the SPD, still officially supported a Socialist/Marxist economic approach, rather than a capitalist society, a widening gap began to open up between the two major players during the period 1949–53. An important milestone in this first phase of development was the result of the second election on 6 September 1953.

5.2   Phase Two

A second CDU/CSU-led coalition government with the FDP, DP and GB/
BHE was formed under Adenauer, who was again elected as Chancellor in
the vote by parliamentarians in Bonn on 9 October 1953, this time with a
61-vote majority. The CDU/CSU popular vote increased by over 15 per cent,
as the SPD vote actually fell very slightly. That widening gap marked the
start of the second phase, a period of hegemony for the Christian Democrats,
characterised above all by the federal election on 15 September 1957, the
only one at which any party obtained over 50 per cent of the vote. That still
remains the case today.

Although strictly speaking no coalition partner was necessary after the 1957
election, it suited Adenauer to retain the tiny DP in his new government (see
1.6.2). The so-called *Adenauerwahl* of 1957, where the CDU/CSU recorded
50.2 per cent of the vote, was almost like a presidential election on Adenauer's
personal popularity. It seemed as if he could do no wrong, with the West
German economic miracle (*Wirtschaftswunder*) bringing tangible benefits for
the voters. On 22 October 1957 Adenauer was again confirmed as Chancellor
in parliament in Bonn – this time with 25 votes to spare.

5.3   Phase Three

The third phase of development marked a period when, despite continued
dominance by the Christian Democrats, the gap between them and the
Opposition began to narrow slightly. The SPD vote was gradually starting to
increase, mainly due to the party's re-alignment via its Godesberg Programme
in 1959, which mentioned neither Marx nor nationalisation policies; instead
the new SPD programme talked of reforming, rather than abolishing, the social
market economy. The Social Democrats started to imagine that one day in
the not-too-distant future it might realistically be able to take over the reins
of power from the ruling Christian Democrats.

At the next federal election on 17 September 1961, for the first time only
three parties cleared the 5 per cent clause. Although the Liberals continued to
offer their services as a government coalition partner to the CDU/CSU, it was
with some reluctance. The FDP tried unsuccessfully to stipulate that Chancellor
Adenauer, at the age of 85, should stand down, but '*der Alte*' refused to do
so. As a result Liberals gained the reputation of a party that had gone back on
its word (*Umfallpartei*), although they claimed at the time to have been let

down by the CSU. The reality was that Adenauer was re-elected Chancellor on 7 November 1961 in the parliamentary vote, but with a majority of only eight votes, leading another CDU/CSU/FDP coalition government. There was, however, an agreement that 'the old man' would stand down half way through the period of legislature in 1963, which is what did in fact happen.

Even though the SPD was of course still in opposition, its electoral performance increased from 31.8 per cent in 1957 to 36.2 per cent in 1961, whilst the CDU vote dropped from 50.2 to 45.3 per cent respectively. So the SPD started to dream of perhaps being able to oust the CDU/CSU from government at some point. That, however, was likely to require the help of a coalition partner, given the principle of PR firmly embedded in the German electoral system, and the FDP was the only other party in the federal parliament following the 1961 election.

5.4   Phase Four

The fourth phase started after Adenauer was at last replaced by Ludwig Erhard as Chancellor on 16 October 1963. Following the federal election on 19 September 1965, Erhard was confirmed in parliament as Chancellor on 20 October 1965. The gap between the two main parties narrowed again, with the Christian Democrats on 47.6 per cent and the Social Democrats now up to their best result so far of 39.3 per cent. In 1961 the FDP also gained its best-ever result at a federal election of 12.8 per cent (this remains its best result at federal level even today), benefitting from a solid portion of '*Leihstimmen*', or borrowed votes, from its senior government partner. It is generally acknowledged that Erhard, although a successful economics minister under Adenauer, was a poor Chancellor. The coalition government soon collapsed – owing to differences between the CDU and the FDP over financial and economic policy and a lack of clear leadership from Erhard, who was replaced by Kurt Georg Kiesinger (CDU). Kiesinger was elected Chancellor with a 91 seat majority on 1 December 1966. A Grand Coalition (*große Koalition*) government was formed between the two big parties, with the CDU providing the Federal Chancellor (Kiesinger) and the SPD the foreign minister (Willy Brandt).

Although this was the first – and so far only – example of such a government (it is always claimed that the politicians themselves view a Grand Coalition as a last resort), it was a very significant development at the time. It gave the SPD its first experience of government responsibility at federal level, and also coincided with a period of real movement in the developing party system, which until then had been dominated by CDU/CSU/FDP cooperation. The tiny FDP now found itself, as the only other party in the *Bundestag*, in splendid isolation on the opposition benches. The Liberals underwent a period of self-examination and re-alignment.

5.5 Phase Five

The fifth phase of development was introduced with the parliamentary election of Willy Brandt as the first postwar SPD Chancellor on 21 October 1969 with a three-vote majority. This followed the sixth federal election on 28 September 1969. The CDU/CSU was still the largest party with 46.1 per cent, but Brandt's Social Democrats (42.7 per cent) formed their first coalition at federal level with the Free Democrats, who paradoxically gained their worst result (5.8 per cent) out of all the 15 federal elections so far. That was probably the price the liberal party had to pay for not having made a clear coalition statement (*Koalitionsausssage*) before the election. Earlier in 1969 some cooperation between the Social Democrats and the Free Democrats had taken place in securing the election of the SPD candidate for Federal President, Gustav Heinemann. This had set the scene for possible teamwork at the level of federal government.

There was some frantic negotiation entered into by Brandt and liberal leader Scheel on election evening and throughout the night. The two party leaders succeeded in bringing about the Federal Republic's first real change in power (*Machtwechsel*), as the FDP transferred its loyalties from one major party to the other. In 1969 the Social Democrats again improved their share of the vote, clearing the 40 per cent mark for the first time. With less than 3.5 per cent separating the two major parties, a new phase in the pattern of federal polls had begun. The SPD was at last the senior partner in a coalition government, with Brandt as Federal Chancellor. That marked the beginning of a new era.

However, the new government soon ran into problems. The Brandt/Scheel partnership tried to push full steam ahead with a policy of *rapprochement* towards the east (*Ostpolitik*). This new policy was controversial, and a number of SPD and FDP politicians left the coalition. It became impossible for Brandt to get legislation through parliament. As a result of the government coalition losing its majority, the parliamentary opposition parties (CDU/CSU) tried to pass the FRG's first constructive vote of no confidence (*das konstruktive*

Misstrauensvotum) in Brandt's government on 27 April 1972, putting forward their candidate for Chancellor, Rainer Barzel. In an extremely tense vote and a situation of high drama, at which one deputy was wheeled into parliament in Bonn on a hospital trolley to cast his vote, and amidst allegations of bribes having being offered to 'buy' politicians' votes, Brandt survived the attempt to pass a constructive vote of no confidence (article 67 of the constitution) in him by just one vote. In the ensuing months it became clear that the only way to resolve the stalemate position was for Brandt to call for a vote of confidence and ask the Federal President to dissolve parliament.

So premature elections (*vorzeitige Wahlen*) had to be called for the first time in the new republic's history, after the government had run only three years of its four-year period of legislature. At the *vorgezogene Wahlen* in November 1972 – the federal elections had originally been scheduled for 1973 – the Social Democrats became, for the first time in the FRG, the largest party, actually out-polling the CDU by a whisker and recording their best federal result of over 45 per cent.

The continuation of a social/liberal government was confirmed when Brandt was returned again as Chancellor by his official election in parliament on 14 December 1972 with a 20-vote majority. The new era in German electoral politics really had been confirmed. Unfortunately for the SPD, the party had a setback to face less than two years later. Willy Brandt took full responsibility and resigned as Chancellor when an East German spy, Günther Guillaume, a member of his personal staff, was arrested in April 1974. On 16 May 1974 Helmut Schmidt (SPD) was elected Chancellor with a parliamentary majority of 18.

5.6 Phase Six

This marked the start of the sixth phase: the new Schmidt/Genscher social/liberal partnership at federal level was to last until 1982. For the 1976 elections all three main parties had new leaders: a young Helmut Kohl was leading the CDU/CSU and Hans-Dietrich Genscher took over the liberal leadership, as Walter Scheel became Federal President. Many observers of the German political scene regarded Schmidt as one of the most competent and gifted chancellors.

Despite some SPD/FDP problems, the political alliance remained intact for the 1980 poll, mainly due to the selection of the controversial CSU leader Franz Josef Strauß as the Chancellor candidate to face Schmidt. There was no love lost between Strauß and the FDP, who actually fought the 1980 campaign on an anti-Strauß ticket. The Greens also contested the election, but the federal party had only just been established, and in any case the polarisation of the fierce Schmidt-Strauß battle for Chancellor meant that they gained a mere 1.5 per cent. Even though the CDU/CSU under Strauß outpolled the SPD (44.5 against 42.9), it was the Christian Democrats' lowest result at federal level since 1949. With the Liberals firmly rejecting any cooperation with Strauß and the Greens nowhere near clearing the 5 per cent hurdle, the social/liberal coalition under Schmidt was returned.

In 1981 and 1982 disagreements surfaced between the government coalition partners over economic policy. The second, and so far only other, constructive vote of no confidence in a sitting German Chancellor was attempted on 1 October 1982. This time the constructive vote of no confidence was successful, as 33 of the FDP delegation transferred their allegiance from Schmidt to Kohl, who was elected in the parliamentary vote by seven votes (he had gained a majority of eleven at a 'rehearsal' the day before). In this way the Schmidt/Genscher government became a Kohl/Genscher government overnight, with Genscher remaining Germany's Foreign Minister. However – and this was very controversial at the time – the change of Federal Chancellor had taken place without the 'blessing' of the electorate.

5.7 Phase Seven

The seventh phase of development began with vociferous demands from several quarters for immediate elections to be held, in order to 'legitimise' the change in power that had occurred. Kohl managed to keep delaying, despite repeated demands from the Strauß and the CSU, until March 1983. By that time the FDP had partially recovered from the shouts of 'disloyalty and treachery' (*Untreue und Verrat*) which had accompanied its *volte-face* six months earlier. In the event, the CDU/CSU increased its share of the vote at the 1983 election to 48.8 per cent, the FDP breathed a sigh of relief, as it managed 6.9 per cent, and the SPD, under its new Chancellor candidate, Hans-Jochen Vogel, slumped to 38.2 per cent. The Greens gained parliamentary representation for the first time on 6 March 1983, with 5.6 per cent and 27 seats in Bonn. Having finally received the democratic approval of the voters, Helmut Kohl was later confirmed as Chancellor by his fellow-parliamentarians (for a second time!) on 29 March 1983, this time with a majority of 21.

In spite of putting forward a new chancellor candidate, Johannes Rau, for the 1987 federal election, the SPD did not succeed in increasing its share of the vote. However the Christian Democrats' vote also dropped from almost 49 per cent in 1983 to just over 44 per cent four years later. The FDP poll improved from 7 per cent to just over 9 per cent, which strengthened its position in the coalition government, and the Greens recorded over 8 per cent in 1987, establishing themselves as a federal party with 42 parliamentary seats, only four fewer than the Liberals. Kohl was confirmed as Chancellor with a four-vote majority in the *Bundestag* on 11 March 1987.

One interesting aspect of this election was the reduced turnout. It was the only federal election to be held in January. The very cold weather in the run-up to the poll on 25 January 1987 must have influenced the turnout. Geoffrey Roberts, in his book *German Politics Today*, points out that the decision to hold the election in January was influenced by the discretionary range of scheduling *Bundestag* elections.[1]

5.8 Phase Eight

The eighth phase of development was initiated by the first all-German federal election on 2 December 1990. The election followed the official process of German Unity on 3 October 1990. The SPD, with their chancellor candidate Oskar Lafontaine, campaigned vigorously for holding the elections before unification, but to no avail. Once the Berlin Wall had fallen (9 November 1989) and German Unity had occurred under the auspices of the Kohl/Genscher government, it was a foregone conclusion that the CDU/CSU/FDP government coalition would be re-elected. Kohl clearly derived tremendous advantage from having been the incumbent who had brought about the unification of the two Germanies. The FDP claimed that much of the credit was also due to Genscher, as Foreign Minister. The liberal party achieved its third best result (11 per cent) with 79 seats.

The election campaign was entirely dominated by just one theme. The atmosphere was one of euphoria and even hysteria over the issue of unification. The first national election for 58 years to be held in a reunited Germany was a landmark in German history and marked the beginning of a new phase in electoral politics. Kohl went down in history as the instigator of German Unity (*Vater der deutschen Einheit*) and was officially confirmed as Chancellor in parliament on 17 January 1990 with an exceptionally big majority of 46.

The electoral system played a key role in the 1990 federal election. A law was passed stating that in order to gain representation in the new all-German parliament a party had to obtain at least 5 per cent of the valid second votes in either the western or the eastern territories. This had two very noticeable effects. Because the West German Greens (*die Grünen*) had not embraced the dominant campaign issue of German Unity, they gained only 4.8 per cent in the west, and therefore no seats in the *Bundestag*. The East German Greens, Alliance '90 (*Bündnis '90*) gained eight seats, on the basis of their performance in the east.

The second effect concerned the newly formed PDS, the Party of Democratic Socialism (*die Partei des demokratischen Sozialismus*). The PDS was the successor to the former East German Socialist Unity party (SED) and, as such, a purely east German phenomenon. It easily cleared the 5 per cent hurdle in the east, but had almost no success at all in the west. Owing to the special ruling for the 1990 election the PDS was allocated 17 parliamentary seats. At the time most observers did not expect the party to return to the *Bundestag* in 1994, when the special electoral ruling would no longer apply.

In 1993 the Greens, in preparation for the forthcoming federal election, formed a single party, *Bündnis '90/die Grünen*, merging the former parties from east and west, and became the first party to return to the *Bundestag* after failing to clear the 5 per cent hurdle four years earlier. The new party gained 7.3 per cent, overtaking the FDP, who surmounted the 5 per cent barrier (6.9 per cent) largely as a result of *Splitting* by CDU supporters. In spite of widespread disillusionment amongst large sections of the electorate, especially in the east, with the government's unfulfilled promises following unification, Kohl still proved marginally more popular than Rudolf Scharping, the latest SPD candidate for chancellor. The CDU/CSU/FDP coalition was returned with a greatly reduced majority of only ten seats. The narrowness of the victory was confirmed when Kohl was re-elected Chancellor in the parliamentary vote on 15 November 1994 by just two votes.

Again there was a reminder at this election of the relevance of the voting system. It had been widely forecast that the PDS would not be represented in the 1994 parliament, given that the 1990 5 per cent ruling applied to the 1990 election only. Whilst it was true that the party was not quite able to comply with the electoral clause for the whole of the territory of the new Germany (PDS 4.4 per cent in 1994), it succeeded in winning four constituency seats, all in East Berlin. Any party that gains at least three direct seats via the constituency vote automatically qualifies for representation in the *Bundestag*. The party was allocated 4.4 per cent of the total number of parliamentary seats (672), which amounted to 29.56 per cent, so 30 seats. Since the PDS did not, however, clear the 5 per cent clause, it was known as a *Bundestagsgruppe*, without the full status of being a parliamentary party (*Fraktion*).

5.9   Phase Nine

The 1998 *Bundestagswahl* heralded the ninth phase of development, as the Kohl era came to an end. This was the first time in the history of the Federal Republic that a sitting chancellor and government was removed from office, unlike the changes in power (*Machtwechsel*) in 1969 and 1982, which involved the FDP as a coalition partner changing sides.

As polling day approached, it began to look as if it really was time for Kohl to go. At the age of 68 and having been Chancellor for 16 years, he would have been well advised *not* to have allowed his name to have gone forward in 1998. Kohl had been Federal Chancellor since 1982, won the federal elections of 1983, 1987 and 1990, becoming the 'father of German Unity,' and still he managed to scrape home again in 1994. Yet after saying publicly (in 1996) that he would not go for the office of Chancellor in 1998, he made the mistake of standing again.

Indeed, there were some opinion polls published by the polling institutes which showed that the CDU/CSU would have stood a better chance of winning in 1998 with a different candidate, although that was a moot point, since Kohl himself had never gone out of his way to promote other leaders in the party whilst he was in charge. This meant that at the time there was a dearth of suitable Christian Democrat candidates to replace Kohl.

On this occasion the SPD put forward the recently elected *Ministerpräsident* of the state of Lower Saxony, Gerhard Schröder, as its chancellor candidate. During the campaign Schröder, an altogether more accomplished media performer, was careful to state that Kohl *had* been a good chancellor (*Kohl war ein guter Kanzler*), and that he *had* brought about German Unity, always using the past tense. The SPD candidate was consistently ranked ahead of the incumbent in terms of who would make the better chancellor. Even some CDU voters preferred Schröder.[2]

With a deteriorating economic situation and mass unemployment, even approaching 20 per cent in the east, the CDU suffered big losses in the 'new' *Länder*. There were some general indications of greater convergence of the two distinctly separate electorates in the east and west, which were already visible at the federal elections of 1990 and 1994, with the exception of the PDS, which was very much an East German party (*die ostdeutsche Volkspartei*). Many voters, especially in the east, had felt badly let down in the period following the all-German elections by Kohl's vision of 'flowering landscapes' (*blühende Landschaften*) and full employment which had failed to materialise. That feeling of disillusionment had been aggravated in the period 1994–98.

The upshot was that on 27 September 1998 a new Schröder/Fischer red/ green government was voted in by the German electorate. It was the first experience of power at federal level for Alliance '90/the Greens, and the first time since the Grand Coalition of 1966–69 that the FDP found itself back on the opposition benches again, since its services as a coalition partner were no longer needed. The PDS cleared the electoral hurdle for the first time (5.1 per cent), thus gaining full status as a *Fraktion*, as well as winning the same four constituencies in East Berlin again. Another new chapter in German politics had commenced.

Notes

1   Geoffrey K. Roberts (2000), *German Politics Today*, Manchester: Manchester University Press, p. 74. The date of 25 January 1987 enabled the next election to be held in the November/December period – it was in fact held in early December 1990. Roberts notes that after that the date of federal elections returned to the more usual and popular time of September/October, which allows the election campaign to take place during the early autumn, after the summer holiday period but still during a time of mild weather and light evenings.

2   Bundestagswahl (1998), *Eine Analyse der Wahl vom 27*, September, Mannheim: Forschungsgruppe Wahlen e.V., pp. 55–63.

Chapter 6

The 2002 Federal Election – A Unique Event

6.1 Election Results: The Photo-finish

The federal election held on 22 September 2002 was unique in the history of the FRG in several respects. It was the first one to be held in Berlin, but more surprisingly it was the first of the 15 postwar federal elections at which the two major parties gained *exactly* the same result – even down to the decimal point! Even though the 'race' was clearly going to be neck-and-neck (*Kopf-an-Kopf*), few were expecting what actually happened: the SPD and CDU/CSU each polled exactly 38.5 per cent of the valid second votes. A tenth phase of the German party system had begun.

The 2002 elections were also unique in staging a live television debate (two in fact) between the chancellor candidates of the two main parties, Schröder and Stoiber. This had never happened before. Another unique aspect of this election was that a third chancellor candidate (Guido Westerwelle, the FDP leader) was put forward, although he was not allowed to appear in the television debates, despite his challenging that decision at the Federal Constitutional Court (*Bundesverfassungsgericht* – BVG). Perhaps of less significance than the above points, but nevertheless unusual, the number of constituencies was reduced from 328 – the new number introduced with the increased territory for the 1990, 1994 and 1998 elections – to 299. That meant of course a reduction in the overall total (as well as the cost) of *Bundestag* deputies to 598.[1]

The role and influence of the German electoral system again moved centre-stage at the 2002 poll. As has been commented on already (see 2.4), not only turnout but also the number of parties allocated parliamentary seats can affect the make-up of the final coalition government. One of the big talking points in the run-up to 22 September 2002 was what was likely to happen to the PDS. Political experts in Germany had confirmed that *with* the post-communist party in the *Bundestag*, i.e. in a five-party system, a coalition government would require 48 per cent of the vote, but only 46 per cent *without* it, i.e. in a four-party system. So just one of the crucial factors which made this federal election one of the tensest ever was the issue of whether the left-wing party of democratic socialism was going to enter the federal parliament or not.

At the first all-German elections in 1990 the PDS had benefited from the application of a dual 5 per cent clause (in either the old or new states). Against expectations, the party again entered the national parliament four years later, owing to its having fulfilled the three-constituency rule. Even though, as expected, it could not obtain 5 per cent of the second vote (4.4 per cent) across the whole of the new Germany, which meant that from 1994 until 1998 the PDS was designated a *Bundestagsgruppe*, but was nevertheless represented by 30 deputies.

In 1998 the PDS returned to the full status of *Fraktion* by surmounting the 5 per cent hurdle (5.1 per cent). Its share of the second vote gave it 35 deputies. It would have qualified for mandates in any case, by virtue of having won the same four constituencies in East Berlin. However the PDS was obviously delighted to have averaged over 5 per cent across Germany, although it remained 'the east German people's party'. It was still extremely popular in the eastern states (19.5 per cent), yet comparatively insignificant as a political force in the west (1.1 per cent).

The situation had changed, however, by September 2002, when only one of the five major German polling institutes was predicting a result of 5 per cent for the party of the left (*die linke Kraft*). Such predictions suggested that success in gaining parliamentary seats at federal level might depend on the constituency vote, but there was a snag. Boundary changes to accommodate the reduction in the number of constituencies from 328 to 299 (see above) meant that the constituencies of Friedrichshain – a PDS stronghold in East Berlin – and Kreuzberg in West Berlin were now part of the new Friedrichshain/Kreuzberg/Prenzlauer Berg-Ost constituency. In the event, the new constituency was actually won by the veteran Green politician Hans-Christian Ströbele, ahead of the SPD, with the PDS candidate coming third.

At the 2002 election the PDS in fact polled 4 per cent of the valid second votes in Germany as a whole, though again only 1.1 per cent in the west, and its vote dropped slightly, somewhat disappointingly, to 16.8 per cent in the east. It won only two constituencies, therefore not qualifying for parliamentary representation on either count.

However, since such direct, constituency seats must always be retained, the Party of Democratic Socialism is now represented in the new *Bundestag* in Berlin by just two deputies: Gesine Lötzsch and Petra Pau, who won the constituencies of Berlin-Lichtenberg/Hohenschönhausen and Berlin-Marzahn/Hellersdorf respectively. The latter used to be held by Gregor Gysi, who did not stand in 2002, although he still campaigned for his party, after standing down over the air miles scandal (*Bonus-Meilen-Affäre*). Some observers felt his resignation over a comparatively trivial matter was not necessary. The PDS certainly lost its star performer, which, in the eyes of many observers, was partly responsible for the party's poor performance. Despite the disappointing result, some analysts feel that the party should not be written off, since it remains in coalition governments in two federal states, Mecklenburg-Vorpommern and Berlin.[2]

6.2 Key Role of the Voting System and the 'Extra' Seats

The PDS result was, however, by no means the only incident which produced great tension on results evening, in an election aptly described as a real nail-biter (*eine richtige Zitterpartie*). The German term *Fotofinish* was used by several politicians during the last few days of the campaign, and it was no exaggeration. When it comes to translating votes into seats, it is the voters' second votes which are counted first. With a voting system based on PR, you would expect two parties with exactly the same percentage of the second vote to be allocated the same number of parliamentary mandates. That is precisely what happened, so Germany's two major parties were initially allocated 247 seats each. Then the first votes, the ones cast for the constituencies, are counted. Once it has been established how many constituencies the parties have gained, that figure is subtracted from the number of list seats. This is where the question of *Überhangmandate*, extra mandates or additional seats (see 2.1) plays an important, in this case vital, part.

On a closer examination of the constituency votes (*Erststimmen*) in 2002, it transpired that the SPD had gained four of the five *Überhangmandate* (one in Hamburg, one in Thuringia and two in Saxony-Anhalt), and the CDU gained one in Saxony. In this way the seat allocation increased to 251 and 248 respectively, amidst protests from the CDU/CSU. Such protests were of course unjustified, given the fact that both major parties have derived advantage from additional mandates in the past and the regulations concerning them had not changed and were clearly stated before the election.

Ironically, Gerhard Schröder, when he was *Ministerpräsident* of Lower Saxony in 1995, applied unsuccessfully to the Federal Constitutional Court in Karlsruhe to get the ruling on additional mandates changed.[3] With hindsight it is fortunate for him and his coalition that he failed in his attempt seven years earlier to change the law! It is for this reason that the new parliament actually contains not the prescribed 598 (299 x 2) deputies (*Abgeordnete*), but in fact 603 (598 plus the five extra seats). In 1990 there were 662 members of parliament (656 plus six extra seats), in 1994 the figure was 672 (656 plus 16 extra seats), and the 1998 *Bundestag* contained 669 deputies (656 plus 13 extra seats).

The Union parties felt that they had really won the 2002 election, because the CDU increased its vote in the west by 3.8 per cent (and 1.1 per cent overall). Add this fact to the CSU increase of 2.2 per cent, and it is easy to understand the feeling of disappointment and even disbelief in CDU/CSU circles. The CSU won every constituency bar one in Bavaria – the SPD candidate Dr Axel Berg won his Munich constituency of *München-Nord* – as well as becoming the third largest party. By contrast, the SPD actually lost 2.4 per cent compared with its 1998 victory. However, another surprise was in store at this unique election when it came to the results for the most likely coalition partners of the two *Volksparteien*.

All five of the major German polling institutes predicted a better result for the FDP than for Alliance '90/the Greens. One of them, Allensbach, actually forecast as much as 13 per cent for the Liberals on one occasion, and many of their predictions for the FDP were in double figures. The polling institutes all got it wrong. Most observers were more than a little surprised when the Greens in fact recorded their best result ever at federal level of 8.6 per cent, ahead of the Free Democrats with 7.4 per cent. This was particularly bad news for the FDP, who had campaigned on a declared aim of reaching 18 per cent (*Strategie 18*).

6.3   Campaign Themes in 2002

One confusing aspect of this particular test of public opinion was that a wide-ranging list of campaign themes was overtaken, almost at the last minute, by two new outstanding, somewhat unusual ones. Until that point in time, there had been no shortage of issues for the 2002 campaign. Apart from the two big questions, always key issues in German federal elections, of who would make the better Chancellor, and which party would be most capable of steering the economy successfully, a number of topics were exercising the voters' minds.

Reducing stubbornly high unemployment was of course one of the most important issues, if not *the* major topic at the start of the 2002 campaign. This took on special significance, given that Gerhard Schröder had made the mistake of saying in September 1998, when he came to office, that he and his party should be judged on their success in tackling the unacceptably high unemployment in Germany, inherited from the Kohl government. Schröder even went as far as to say that he and his party would not deserve to be re-elected if he and his government did not significantly reduce Germany's unemployment figures.[4]

Polls had been conducted at which up to 80 per cent of those questioned had named unemployment as the most important campaign issue. That must have seemed like a gift to the opposition parties. However, Edmund Stoiber, although he frequently attacked the incumbent Chancellor on the government's record during the two television debates, failed to spell out what his own approach to tackling unemployment would be.

Important topics such as education, global economic policy, social justice, tax reform, the environment, pension provision and the integration of foreigners into German society were all cast aside when the most important of two crucial factors in influencing the outcome of the contest occurred. In early August appalling floods devastated the country, first in the east, then affecting the west too, causing one of Germany's worst-ever catastrophes.

As the ruling Federal Chancellor/head of government Schröder was able to be seen in a statesmanlike role managing a national crisis, thus deriving benefit from the *Kanzlerbonus*. The successful management of the *Flutkatastrophe* helped both the Chancellor's SPD, as well as the Greens, with their emphasis on getting the right balance between economy and ecology. Stoiber and the opposition parties were slow to react; in fact they singularly failed to get to grips with the floods issue, as did the PDS, even though it was initially a predominantly east German concern.

The other crucial factor turning the tables in favour of the government parties was Schröder's decision to adopt a policy, apparently supported by a majority of the population, of refusing to send German soldiers to Iraq in the event of a war, regardless of what the UN or US decided. Stoiber was forced into formulating his own policy on this issue. He came up with the statement of not 'going it alone' (*kein Alleingang*), which seemed rather half-hearted by comparison. The question of the floods was the more important, but expert observers in Germany came to the clear conclusion that the two issues of *Flut und Frieden* – floods and peace (in Iraq) – had swung the election for the government coalition parties. The German news magazine *der Spiegel* reported that, had it not been for these two issues, the election evening could easily have ended up in disaster for the SPD and the Greens.[5]

The Greens were allocated 55 seats, eight more than in the last parliament, as against 47 for the FDP (43 in 1998), and this boosted the SPD majority of just three seats over its rivals, the CDU/CSU, to a nine-seat majority for the new red/green coalition government. So, despite having been returned to office in 2002, Chancellor Schröder did not find himself in a strong position. At the time of the election several cartoonists and political commentators expressed the opinion that the SPD had crossed the finishing line on the backs of the Greens. With such a narrow majority in the *Bundestag,* and no majority at all in the *Bundesrat*, the political outlook for the second red/green federal coalition in the autumn of 2002 was not rosy. The SPD finance minister, Hans Eichel, faced several challenges in the areas of taxation, pensions and revenue in general.

A closer examination of the 2002 results reveals that the election was really won in the east. Although this was the fourth federal election since German Unity, the figures for the western and eastern territories still show marked differences. The electoral turnout was higher in the west (80.7 per cent) than in the east (72.9 per cent). The SPD gained only 38.3 per cent of the second votes in the west, a loss of 4 per cent against 1998, yet won almost 40 per cent in the east (2 per cent more than in 1998). This contrasted with the position of the Christian Democrats, who achieved 40.8 per cent in the west, more than its chief rivals the Social Democrats, but could manage only 28.3 per cent in the east.

Despite the comparatively strong performance of the Union parties overall in 2002, it should nevertheless be remembered that its increased vote was almost entirely in the southern *Länder* of Bavaria (CSU) and Baden-Württemberg (CDU). So the CDU/CSU improved their electoral performance in the south of the Federal Republic, but not in the north or the east.[6]

In addition to the key role of the electoral system and the related question of additional mandates, there was a sense in which the 2002 poll was greatly influenced by political personalities. First, there was the *Kanzlerfrage*, the Schröder/Stoiber battle, already referred to above. The Chancellor question was given an added dimension this time by the inclusion of a third candidate in the shape of the FDP leader, Guido Westerwelle, even though there was never really any realistic possibility of his becoming Chancellor.

Westerwelle was also a controversial personality within his own party, and his battles, and those of his party, with Jürgen W. Möllemann (over his alleged anti-semitic remarks contained in some flyers he published) made headline news, as did the whole *Strategie 18* policy of the liberal party. Möllemann had been a leading light behind the conviction that the FDP had a serious chance of attaining 18 per cent of the second vote. In practice that was just about as unlikely as Westerwelle becoming the German chancellor.

The resignation of the charismatic Gregor Gysi from the Berlin *Land* government also played a decisive role in the fortunes of the PDS. A dynamic and persuasive speaker, seen by many as the real star of his party, Gysi has so often in the past had an influence on the results of the party representing east German interests.

The most popular politician in the campaign was Joschka Fischer. He undoubtedly played a crucial role in the achievement by Alliance 90/the Greens of their best federal result so far. The West German Green Party in particular often used to argue against the promotion of an individual personality to promote the party, saying that policies were more important than personalities. Nevertheless, in the 2002 federal election campaign there is no doubt that the personal popularity and appeal of Fischer was indeed a bonus to both his own party and the return to power of the coalition.

6.4   Electoral Behaviour in Germany

In terms of voter realignment, the 2002 election confirmed some, though not all, of the general trends in voting patterns that are firmly entrenched in German electoral behaviour. As far as the question of religious cleavage is concerned, there has always been a clear tendency for Catholic voters in Germany on the whole being more likely to support the CDU/CSU. Protestant (*evangelisch*) voters and those with no links to the Church have usually been more likely to support the SPD, although the Catholic/conservative party link is stronger than the Protestant/SPD link.

This also explains why the Christian Democrats did badly in the east, where the majority of voters are termed *konfessionslos* in German, i.e. have no strong link with any denomination. The eastern territories always had relatively few Catholics, and the former GDR was really a Protestant area, although the country was considered to have been 'de-christianised' to a large extent by the regime. However, two factors should be emphasised straight away regarding the influence of the denominational dimension on electoral behaviour in German politics.

Firstly, the above trend increases dramatically amongst regular church-goers (*regelmäßige Kirchengänger*). It decreases amongst those Catholics who attend mass only once a month, and decreases sharply amongst those who attend church only occasionally, perhaps only for baptisms, marriages and funerals. An analysis by the Mannheim polling institute *Forschungsgruppe Wahlen* reveals that although the CDU/CSU gained 38.5 per cent of the vote in 2002 overall, it received 52 per cent from Catholics generally, and as much as 73 per cent from regular church-going Catholics.[7] The SPD, who of course also gained 38.5 per cent overall, gained below-average support (approximately 30 per cent) from Catholic voters.

There is also evidence (for example in southern Germany) that regular church-goers, whether Catholic or Protestant are more likely to vote CSU in Bavaria, or indeed CDU in Baden-Württemberg. It is therefore regular church attendance, rather than simply church membership, i.e. simply having been baptised a Catholic or a Protestant, that is the key factor here.

Secondly, such links, although they still exist, were stronger in the 1950s and 1960s (in what was then West Germany) than nowadays. In those days the Catholic Church still required all priests to read a pastoral letter (*Hirtenbrief*) from the pulpit of every Catholic church on the Sunday before a federal election, recommending Catholics to support a *Christian* party. There were not too many with the term *christlich* in their party name!

In Germany's present more secular and pluralist society, the links between the population and the two established German churches are now weaker than they used to be, though still clearly evident. It is calculated that, amongst Germany's current population of some 82 million, there are over 28 million Protestants and more than 27 million Catholics. It should, however, not be forgotten that these figures include everyone who is nominally a member of either of the churches, but not necessarily a regular attendee at church.

Another factor to be remembered is that in Germany membership of one of the two main churches is related to the payment of church taxes (*Kirchensteuer*). Although some German citizens do go through the official process of ex-communicating themselves from the Church in which they have been brought up, in order to avoid paying the church taxes, this is felt by many to be a very big step, which not everyone wishes to take.

At the 2002 federal election the question of religious cleavage, and its effect on voting patterns, was still evident. The Union parties, as usual, gained more support from Catholics than Protestants (53:38) and the Social Democrats obtained more votes from Protestants than Catholics (41:29). So the denominational dimension was still a factor, though by no means the only one, in giving some indication of how German voters might behave at an election.

A second general indicator of voting patterns affecting the two major parties is to be found in the area of the urban/rural split. In terms of where the voters live, the SPD has always done well in urban areas, whilst the Union parties usually perform better in rural constituencies. This tendency has been confirmed over many years in just about every analysis of voting behaviour, right down to local level. Again there was confirmation of this trend at the 2002 federal election: the rural vote was 43:37 in favour of the CDU/CSU, with a 40:30 figure to the advantage of the Social Democrats in urban areas.

A third category where an established trend in electoral behaviour continues is the age factor. The SPD no longer attracts as many young voters as it once used to (the same applies to the Greens too), although in 2002 the SPD did receive more votes form German *Jungwähler* (18–24 year-olds) than its chief rivals, the CDU/CSU (39:22). One factor which has remained constant is the greater likelihood of voters aged over 60 giving their support to the CDU/CSU. At the national poll in 2002 the Union parties again gained a slightly greater share of the vote cast by those over 60 (45:39). So, in terms of age of voter, the SPD received support more or less equally from all age groups, though they did slightly better amongst the 45–59 category (38 per cent). The CDU/CSU did best in the over-60 group (46 per cent) and worst amongst the 18–24 year-olds (32 per cent).[8]

However, the established trend whereby more female than male voters normally support the Christian Democrats did not apply on 22 September 2002. Unusually, slightly more men than women supported the CDU/CSU, although the differences were not great (41:38 per cent), and the SPD gained rather more votes from women than men, although the opposite is often the case.

Another unexpected development in 2002 was that the SPD lost some of its traditional support from manual workers (*Arbeiter*), who are frequently 'very strongly associated with membership of a trade union',[9] and therefore reliable SPD voters. The SPD also lost some of the support it had gained from salaried employees (*Angestellte*) at the previous federal election. Both those groups were strong SPD-voters in 1998, and manual workers and trade union members have normally formed a section of the electorate offering hard-core support for the Social Democrats over the years at elections in Germany. In general terms, the CDU/CSU normally gains more votes in areas where agriculture plays an important role, as well as in the services sector.

As far as profession is concerned, structural changes in German society occurred between 1950 and 2000. The number of manual workers (*Arbeiter*) decreased from 51 to 35 per cent during that 50-year period. The number of self-employed (*Selbstständige*) also decreased from 28 to 11 per cent, whilst the number of salaried employees (*Angestellte*) and civil servants (*Beamte*) increased from 21 to 55 per cent over the same period.

These changes have affected voting patterns. Whilst manual workers in Germany and members of a trade union – just over half of trade union members still voted for the SPD in 2002 – have traditionally supported the Social Democrats (see above), and still do, there have been considerable losses. Although more salaried employees gave their support to the SPD than to their chief rivals, it was the Christian Democrats who derived more electoral support from civil servants (41:33).[10]

Notes

1   In fact the total number of members of the new *Bundestag* was 603, owing to five extra seats (*Überhangmandate*). Nevertheless, this was a significant reduction compared with the numbers who entered the German parliament after the federal elections of 1990, 1994 and 1998: 662, 672 and 669 respectively.

2   This point was made by Hugh Williamson on p. 2 of a special World Report on Germany in the *Financial Times* on 25 November 2002.

3   Reported by *der Spiegel* in an election special edition, *Wahlsonderheft '02* on 29 September 2002.

4   'Wenn wir es nicht schaffen, die Arbeitslosenquote signifikant zu senken, dann haben wir es weder verdient wiedergewählt zu werden, noch werden wir wiedergewählt' ('If we do not succeed in reducing unemployment significantly, then we will neither deserve to be re-elected, nor will we be re-elected').

5   'Ohne die eindringlichen Töne zu den Themen Flut und Frieden wäre der Wahlabend für Schröder vermutlich ein Desaster gewesen' ('Without the vivid emphasis of the key issues of the floods and peace (in Iraq) the election evening would presumably have been a disaster for Schröder'), *Spiegel Wahlsonderheft '02*, 24 September 2002, p. 11.

6   As a result of this state of affairs it was expected that Edmund Stoiber's CSU would attempt to increase its influence in the CDU/CSU partnership, after its strong showing in the 2002 elections. This point was made by Hugh Williamson in his article on p. 2 of a special World Report on Germany in the Financial Times on 25 November 2002.

7   Bundestagswahl (2002), *Eine Analyse der Wahl vom 22*, September, Mannheim: Forschungsgruppe Wahlen e.V., p. 64.

8   All figures taken from the *Spiegel* special edition *Wahlsonderheft '02*, 29 September 2002, p. 42.

9   William E. Paterson and David Southern (1991), Governing Germany, Oxford: Blackwell, p. 178.

10   See op. cit., Forschungsgruppe Wahlen, 2002, pp. 55–62.

Chapter 7

Influence of the Electoral System on the Party System and Individual Parties

7.1 The Federal Party System

In Germany, as in other countries, the nature and development of the electoral system has been intertwined with that of the party system (see Introduction). As has been clearly demonstrated, different German methods of voting, from the Prussian system onwards (see 1.1) have brought very different influences and pressures to bear. Even the 'perfect' proportional representation method employed in the Weimar Republic had its shortcomings (see 1.3). Whilst the Weimar electoral system did not create the problems which obtained in the German polity of that time, it certainly reinforced some of them.[1]

It was for this reason that considerable care was taken over the way in which the West German electoral system was designed and regulated during the initial postwar period (1945–49), culminating in the first federal electoral law, passed on 15 June 1949 (see 1.6). The political instability, fragmentation and the chaotic situation caused by a plethora of splinter parties between 1919 and 1933, followed by the negative experiences under the National Socialist German Workers Party (NSDAP) between 1933 and 1945, had to be avoided at all costs. The way to achieve that was seen at the time to be by the establishment of a new party system supported by a new electoral system.

The concept of a party system includes the notion of the relationships between several parties and assumes the existence of free and fair elections to ascertain the will of the people, as well as a competitive element where a change of power at the highest level of government is possible. Definitions of the basic concept of a party system usually also entail reference to an organisational framework that encompasses a strong aspect of stability and choice.

Elements such as the type of governance – parliamentary versus presidential, federalist versus unitary – play an important role, as do the proper representation of interest groups and the ability to deal fairly with societal conflicts. In a federal set-up, which implies a decentralised system, in which there is real power-sharing, divided between a central government and several regional ones, the German concept of unity in diversity (*Einheit in Vielfalt*) is normally seen as a strength, although there can be some disadvantages to it as well. The periodic debate concerning the German education system, under which the federal states enjoy cultural sovereignty (*Kulturhoheit der Länder*) is just one instance of possible reforms under consideration. On the whole, the verdict on the German federal system, with its implications for the political system, is now overwhelmingly a positive one, despite recent concerns that there is perhaps a danger of transferring too many powers to the federation (*Bund*).

After German Unity in 1990, it became very clear, very quickly, that the differing political cultures of east and west were not going to be united overnight. It was often more accurate to speak of two German party systems: a four-party system in the western territories (SPD, CDU/CSU, Greens, FDP) and a three-party system in the eastern states (SPD, CDU/CSU, PDS). Whilst the PDS is the most obvious example of a party whose influence is extremely significant in the east yet negligible in the west, the 2002 election results confirm that that is by no means the full story.

Above all, a party system and an electoral system must be capable of functioning effectively (*arbeitsfähig*). By providing the historical context and examining the gradual postwar development process of the German electoral system, it has been demonstrated that the party system moved from what looked like a nascent multi-party system to the current one, in which two major political forces and two smaller ones are now firmly established. It has to be said, however, that initially in West Germany the emerging party system was strongly influenced by one Federal Chancellor (Adenauer) and one particular party (CDU/CSU).

Nevertheless the method of voting ensured that coalition governments[2] were likely to be formed in the early years of the Federal Republic; this led, in general terms, to two or three political parties often having to work together at federal level and go for consensus rather than conflict. As we have seen, by 1961 a clear three-party system had emerged at federal level. Not only did the federal parliament contain only three parties between 1961 and 1982 (see 2.2), but amazingly at the 1976 federal election 99 per cent of the valid second votes were cast for those three parties.[3]

Indeed the survival of the third party, the liberal FDP, was due in no small measure to the Federal Republic's voting system. The continued presence of the Liberals was welcomed by those German voters who valued and supported the benefits of cooperation and consensus, as they saw it, being brought about by the election of a coalition government. Some electors preferred voting for a coalition government, rather than the alternating 'seesaw' politics of a two-party system, which, as in the United Kingdom and the United States, can sometimes become simply a matter of exchanging government and opposition parties.

It was, however, also criticised by some observers who viewed the tiny Free Democratic Party as one that had a disproportionate amount of power and influence in the West German party system, beyond its real size and importance, in terms of what the party stood for. The FDP was sometimes accused of being opportunistic, always with an eye open to the main chance, obsessed with remaining in power, adapting its loyalty to either of the two main parties at will. It was in this context that the German phrase *Opportunistenpartei ohne Profil* (a party of opportunists with no clear image) was sometimes used to describe the Free Democrats at various periods between 1960 and 1990.

In the present political situation in Germany the Liberals, of course, no longer occupy the pivotal position in the party system which they once did. That unusual position was emphasised particularly in 1969 and 1982 when the FDP engineered the two major changes in power (*Machtwechsel*) at federal level.

The Free Democratic Party was able to adopt four clear functions in the West German party system. These included playing a pivotal role, firstly by offering its services as a majority maker (*Mehrheitsmacher*), as a coalition partner for either of the two main parties (SPD or CDU/CSU). Its second function was that of a liberal corrective (*liberales Korrektiv*), a sort of political watchdog to prevent the more extreme elements in the Christian Democrats or the Social Democrats from straying too far to the Right or Left. Thirdly, the FDP succeeded in promoting itself as an agent of transition, with the ability to enable a change in power (*Machtwechsel*) at federal level. Fourthly, the Free Democrats tried hard to promote an image of themselves as an ideological or numerical balancer in the party system. In this way the German Liberals claimed to stand for providing an element of moderation, balance and continuity in (west) German politics. These roles and functions are nowadays no longer available to the FDP in the current German party system.

In fact the Liberals, although still represented in the federal parliament in Berlin, nowadays find themselves on the opposition benches; the crucial turning point was when the new, united Green Party (Alliance 90/the Greens) first formed a federal coalition government with the SPD in 1998, and the same partnership was repeated in 2002. Once the Greens were able to offer their services as a viable coalition partner at federal level, the position of the FDP in the federal party system was considerably weakened.

Nevertheless, this does not detract from the continuing benefits that the electoral system offers the German voter. The two-vote system continues to enable voters in a federal election to split their votes, if they so desire, and to cast their ballot in favour of a government coalition. It also continues to encourage the emergence of new political groupings, should they gather sufficient support amongst the population, given the relevance of the proportional element in the formation of governments at both federal and regional levels.

The German party system, assisted by a workable, functioning electoral system, based on proportional representation, proved itself over the years to be capable of adapting and developing. Just as the established three-party system, between 1961 and 1982, was beginning to look to some observers as if it was becoming 'stale' and boring, the West German Green Party (*die Grünen*) arrived on the national political stage, clearing the 5 per cent hurdle at federal level for the first time in 1983. That event certainly succeeded in 'shaking things up' by creating a four-party system and a federal parliament that experienced some changes.

With the advent of German Unity in 1990 the 'new' German party system again showed itself to be capable of adapting to the prevailing political circumstances, again assisted and underpinned by the electoral system. A special amendment was made to the electoral law. It was valid for the 1990 all-German elections only, whereby a party had to satisfy the 5 per cent clause in *either* the territory of the former FRG *or* that of the former GDR. The German voting system again proved to be an essential and positive constituent part of the party system. In practice it meant that the amendment was responsible for offering seventeen parliamentary seats to the PDS, the Party of Democratic Socialism, representing almost exclusively the political interests of German voters in the east. In 1990 a four-party system became a five-party system: CDU/CSU, SPD, FDP, Alliance 90/the Greens, PDS.

At the national polls of 1990, 1994, 1998 and 2002 an almost forgotten aspect of Germany's electoral system – the three-constituency alternative to gaining at least 5 per cent of the total valid second votes – was highlighted again. The PDS benefited from winning four constituencies in east Berlin in 1994 and 1998 – three would have sufficed (see 1.6) – but in 2002 it managed to gain only two constituencies via the first votes and failed to secure 5 per cent of the second votes. As a result the PDS, despite having been part of the five-party system following the elections of 1990, 1994 and 1998, did not enter the *Bundestag* in 2002, except for Gesine Lötzsch and Petra Pau, the two PDS candidates who won their constituencies (see 6 above).

7.2   Individual Parties

7.2.1   The CDU/CSU

The right-of-centre Christian Democratic Union (CDU) was quick to establish itself in the new postwar party system. Both the CDU and its Bavarian sister party, the Christian Social Union (CSU), were eager to represent basic Christian values, as a strong counter reaction to what had happened during the political system dominated by Hitler and National Socialism. The CSU, under the chairmanship of first Alfons Goppel and later Franz Josef Strauß, wanted to promote specific Bavarian interests and yet still cooperate in parliament with the CDU. The CSU, though it forms a joint parliamentary party with the CDU, is an independent party, founded in Bamberg, Würzburg and various parts of Bavaria in the autumn of 1945, and then officially at *Land* level on 8 January 1946.[4] Nevertheless, its origins can be traced back to the Bavarian Patriot Party (*Bayerische Patriotische Partei*) of 1869 and the Catholic Centre Party (*Zentrum*) from 1887 onwards.

Political Catholicism during the Weimar Republic was represented by the German Centre Party, and in Bavaria by the Bavarian People's Party (*Bayerische Volkspartei – BVP*). This party was the immediate predecessor of the CSU, which as the German newspaper *die Welt* once put it, was made of 'a different wood' from the CDU.[5] Together the CDU/CSU derived great prestige and benefit from the new postwar electoral system and the federal elections that took place in the early years of the Federal Republic.

Although the Christian Democratic parties were originally in favour of a first-past-the-post method of voting during the period 1945–49, they recorded impressive results under the PR system, went from strength to strength after each of the first three federal elections, and rapidly became the dominant force in West German politics. Konrad Adenauer, the first Federal Chancellor of the FRG – he was elected by his fellow parliamentarians in 1949 by just one vote (his own) – and his centre-right, conservative party were soon holding sway over a new, successful polity, so desperately sought by the German people. The new political system was soon underpinned by the West German economic miracle (*Wirtschaftswunder*). In West Germany in the early 1950s the only way to go was 'up', taking zero hour (*die Stunde Null*) as the starting-point. As the economic boom continued, a period of tremendous growth in the Federal Republic was experienced and the 1957 federal election was described as the 'Adenauer election' (*die Adenauerwahl*), since the first Federal Chancellor and his party were widely associated with the increased standard of living.

At the time there really seemed to be no realistic alternative to returning Chancellor Adenauer, his economics minister Ludwig Erhard, the so-called 'father of the economic miracle' and the CDU/CSU to power. Their popular appeal, in electoral terms, shot up from 31 per cent in 1949 to 45.2 in 1953, and even cleared the 50 per cent mark in 1957 (the only occasion right up to the present day when this has happened).

If the 1957 federal election seemed more like a referendum on the personal popularity of Adenauer and his party, some of the Bavarian state elections sometimes seemed more like referenda on Franz Josef Strauß and his party. Strauß, who was Chairman of the CSU from 1961 until the day he died in 1988 and minister-president of the Free State of Bavaria (*der Freistaat Bayern*) from 1978 until 1988, was the uncrowned 'king' of Bavaria. Under his 'reign' the CSU perfected what the prolific writer on Bavarian politics, Professor Alf Mintzel called a political dual role (*eine politische Doppelrolle*): the Bavarian party of state played not only a crucial role as a regional party (*Landespartei*) but also played a key role as part of a federal party (*Bundespartei*), namely the CDU/CSU in Bonn.

The CSU derived even greater advantage from the German electoral process than its sister party, the CDU. At the federal election of 1976 the CSU gained 60 per cent of the vote in Bavaria, and in 1974 the party managed to amass 62.1 per cent of the vote at the Bavarian state election (*bayerische Landtagswahl*). At the Bavarian elections of 1986 the author personally witnessed Strauß at a rally in Munich two days before the vote predicting a result for the CSU of '55 per cent plus x'. On polling day the CSU gained a staggering 55.8 per cent.

Only once did the close CDU/CSU relationship look as if it might cease. In November 1976, following the federal election, during which disagreements between the two sister parties reached a head and Strauß was openly critical of Kohl. FJS blamed Chancellor candidate Kohl for the victory of the SPD under Schmidt. The CSU voted by 30 to 18 in a secret ballot, at its meeting in Wildbad Kreuth in Upper Bavaria, in favour of terminating the long-standing agreement over the formation of a joint parliamentary party (*Fraktionsgemeinschaft*) in the *Bundestag*.[6] The traditional bastions of CSU support in Old Bavaria adopted a hard-line attitude; however, Kohl fought back fiercely, by threatening to allow the CDU to campaign in Bavaria. The split, which could have been potentially very damaging for both parties, was healed on 12 December 1976, just two days before the new German parliament was due to convene.

After a brief period in the doldrums, following the death of F.J. Strauß in October 1988, the CSU regained its position of hegemony in Bavaria and recovered its special position (*Sonderstellung*) in the German polity. Under minister president Edmund Stoiber (he has been in power in Munich since 1993), the CSU now dominates elections and electoral politics again. In 2002 Stoiber became only the second CSU leader since 1949 to be put forward as the CDU/CSU chancellor candidate for a federal election (the only other one was of course Strauß in 1980).

The September 2002 contest was incredibly close (see 6.1) and there is no doubt that Stoiber, when the results appeared on election evening, thought he had won. Even a few months after the federal election, in January 2003, his popularity continued, as he overtook Chancellor Schröder in the regular monthly Spiegel questionnaire (*Umfrage*).[7]

The CDU, after the narrow defeat at the 2002 national poll, recovered ground dramatically by winning an absolute majority of the seats at the first two tests of public opinion to be held since the federal election. At the regional elections (*Landtagswahlen*), held on 2 February 2003, the CDU replaced the SPD in Schröder's home federal state of Lower Saxony. The Christian Democrat challenger Christian Wulff spectacularly defeated the SPD minister president Sigmar Gabriel. On the same day Roland Koch (CDU), the ruling minister president of Hesse, also gained a landslide victory. Four years earlier he had needed the support of the FDP, but in 2003 that was no longer necessary, although the Liberals increased their share of the vote in both federal states.

As usual, analysis of the *Land* elections investigated the question of whether regional (*Landespolitik*) or federal politics (*Bundespolitik*) had played the dominant role in the voters' decision. In fact the answer was both. Whilst regional and local concerns had been relevant, the background of German unemployment rising to 4.6 million and the SPD's handling of the economy, health and pensions influenced voting behaviour too. In December 2000 the membership of the CDU was just over 616,000. That of the CSU was given as just over 178,000.

7.2.2   The SPD

The origins of Germany's oldest political party, the Social-Democratic Party of Germany, can be traced back to the workers' association (*Allgemeiner deutscher Arbeiterverein*), founded in 1863 by Ferdinand Lasalle, and the social-democratic workers' party, founded in 1869 by Bebel and Liebknecht, which became the socialist workers' party of Germany (*Sozialistische Arbeiterpartei Deutschlands*) in 1875. Owing to the way the party had suffered state persecution under the Socialist Law (1878–90) and also its 'unfair' representation in the Weimar Republic (see 1.3 and 1.4), the SPD was a major supporter of a voting system based on proportionality when the design of a new electoral system for West Germany was discussed at the meetings of the Parliamentary Council in 1948/49.

Despite the very close result of the first federal election in 1949 (CDU/CSU 31.0 – SPD 29.2 per cent), the SPD was relegated to the role of opposition party at once; it was unable to shake off this newly acquired label, as the major party of government (CDU/CSU, see above) increased its share of the popular vote to 45.2 and 50.2 per cent in 1953 and 1957 respectively. At those polls the SPD disastrously recorded less than one third of the vote.

It was not until the SPD introduced its *Godesberger Programme* at its party conference in Bad Godesberg in 1959, when it officially ceased to be a Marxist party, which had always been always associated with anti-clericalism, that it started to narrow the electoral gap between its main rivals, the Christian Democrats, and itself. The SPD had also been assisted by the banning in 1956 of the communist KPD.

During the 1950s the SPD found it very difficult to compete with its main political rivals, the CDU/CSU, who were presiding over a period of unprecedented economic growth in the newly established state of West Germany. However, at the federal polls of 1961 and 1965 the Social Democrats did manage to improve their results (36.2 and 39.3 per cent respectively). The SPD had begun to embrace the concept of the social market economy and started to widen its appeal, especially amongst manual workers and trade union members in urban areas such as the Ruhr and the Saarland, and cities such as Berlin, Hamburg and Bremen. The key players in the SPD reform movement were Herbert Wehner, Willy Brandt and Helmut Schmidt. Another leading politician was Karl Schiller, who was spectacularly successful as the SPD economics minister in the late 1960s. Their leadership qualities and invaluable advice on how to surmount the electoral barriers facing German social democracy ensured that the SPD was not going to reside in the '30 per cent ghetto' forever. Changes were needed in the areas of commitment to NATO, foreign policy, relations with the Churches and the whole question of the public image of the party.

The SPD's long march back to power was helped by participation in the Grand Coalition (*Große Koalition*) government 1966–69, pre-empted by the Federal Republic's first economic slump and the failure of Erhard's government. Even when the SPD finally succeeded in providing the Federal Chancellor for the first time (Willy Brandt in 1969), they were still marginally out-polled by the CDU/CSU. Yet the party derived great benefit from the West German political system in general, and its electoral system in particular. The encouragement offered by allowing the German electorate to opt for a coalition government if they so wished, facilitated a change of power, deemed necessary by many voters after some 20 years of CDU dominance. The change in power (*Machtwechsel*) in Bonn came in the form of a new social-liberal partnership, which was able to take over the reigns of power at federal level.

The SPD/FDP coalition government remained in power from 1969 until 1982, although the only occasion when the SPD was the largest party in the *Bundestag* was in 1972. Brandt's strong personal appeal and impressive performances by other government ministers produced an increase in the parliamentary majority from 12 to almost 50 seats. The long march to power for the SPD, getting out of the so-called '30 per cent ghetto' of the 1950s, was over. It was, however, not without its downside.

The move towards the centre ground, where the majority of the votes are to be found, brought criticism from the Young Socialists (*Jusos*), as well as from older Marxists from the trade union movement.[8] The achievement of providing the largest parliamentary party in the *Bundestag*) was not repeated until 1998, when the SPD returned to political power after 16 years of rule by Helmut Kohl and the Christian Democrats. 1972 and 1998 are the only two national polls so far, at which the Social Democrats have gained more votes than any other party.

Despite a slight disproportionately on the Loosemore-Hanby index in German elections (100 per cent proportionality is virtually unobtainable in practice),[9] the PR dimension, with its 5 per cent clause, enabled the Social Democrats to make a much greater contribution to the political system of the Federal Republic than to those of earlier German systems. The return to government responsibility and electoral success for the Social Democrats was accompanied by Brandt's policy of *rapprochement* with the East (*Ostpolitik*).

Unfortunately for the SPD, its election results, having reached a peak in 1972, began to fall from 1976 onwards. After Schmidt was replaced by Kohl by means of the Federal Republic's only successful vote of no confidence (*das konstruktive Misstrauensvotum*) so far in October 1982, the 1983 premature federal election brought the worst result for the Social Democrats for nearly 20 years, only marginally better than its 1965 poll of 39.3 per cent. Things got worse four years later, as the party gained its lowest vote in 1987 since 1961, and the 1989/90 unification process appeared to take the SPD somewhat by surprise and left the party divided, as Helmut Kohl and the Christian Democrats went from strength to strength, deriving great political prestige from the whole German unity issue.

The federal election on 27 September 1998 was of great significance, as the CDU/CSU recorded its worst election result since 1949. A sitting chancellor was voted out of office for the first time in the history of the FRG, the SPD became the largest party in the federal parliament for only the second time at postwar elections (see above), and the Green Party (*Bündnis 90/die Grünen*) offered its services as a coalition partner in a federal government for the first time ever. There can be no doubt that the way in which the SPD orchestrated its election campaign, employing a new advertising agency and adopting a very high media profile strategy, helped the party to victory via the approach of deriving maximum advantage from the German political and electoral systems.

The narrowest of victories in 2002, as we have seen, returned the Schröder/Fischer partnership to power in Berlin. Yet the new government's perceived poor handling of the German economy influenced the results of the first regional elections in February 2003. With only 33.4 per cent of the vote in Chancellor Schröder's home state of Lower Saxony, the SPD was ejected from power in Hanover. On the same day the CDU retained power in Hesse, improving their position by gaining an absolute majority of the seats in Wiesbaden; it was the worst SPD result (29.1 per cent) in Hesse since 1945. The electoral position of the Social Democrats only four months after the federal poll was described in the German press as catastrophic. Words like 'disaster' and 'double debacle' were used to sum up the SPD performances in the two *Land* elections. The landslide victories for the CDU in both polls did more than just give the SPD 'something to think about' (*einen Denkzettel verpassen*).

In December 2000 the membership of the SPD was just under 735,000.

7.2.3   The FDP

The Free Democratic Party (*die Freie Demokratische Partei*) was founded as a new, single liberal party in Heppenheim in 1948. The history of German liberalism can be traced back to the German Progressive Party (*Deutsche Fortschrittspartei*) of Virchow and Mommsen in 1861. The formation of the National Party only five years later marked the beginning of a long and enduring split in the liberal movement. The two directions were continued in the Weimar Republic, with two liberal parties: the German People's Party (*die Deutsche Volkspartei* – DVP) and the German Democratic Party (*die Deutsche Demokratische Partei* – DDP). For this reason the establishment of a single liberal party in western Germany in 1948 was heralded as a major achievement.

However there were in fact considerable differences of emphasis on the precise definition of liberal policy in the different western states. Right-wing liberalism, the defender of more nationalist, free market economic interests, found resonance in North Rhine Westphalia and Hesse. The more left-wing, liberal-democratic orientation was particularly associated with Baden-Württemberg, as well as Hamburg and Bremen.

In fact Ludwig Erhard, Adenauer's economics minister and so-called 'father of the economic miracle', was a Protestant from Fürth in Central Franconia, Bavaria; he was termed a 'would-be liberal' (*ein verhinderter Liberaler*) by the Bavarian FDP. Erhard, a professor of economics and advocate of a liberal, social market economy, certainly was not keen to become a member of the CSU and in fact did not make a decision about joining any party until relatively late. He eventually opted for the CDU.

Up until the mid-1960s the national liberal wing of the FDP dominated, in spite of the Spiegel Affair (1962) producing permanent damage to the CSU/FDP relationship; after the occasional run-in with the CDU/CSU and the sobering experience of sitting alone on the opposition benches in Bonn during the period of the Grand Coalition (1966–69), the liberal democratic wing gained prominence. This was accompanied by participation in federal government with the SPD, as Brandt became the first SPD Chancellor since 1930.

In the 1980s the free-market orientation re-emerged, coinciding with a re-alignment in FDP circles with CDU economic policy. In 1982 the Liberals transferred their allegiances back to a coalition government at federal level with the Christian Democrats. This remained the case from 1982 until 1998. During that period the FDP provided the foreign minister, giving the liberal party considerable influence over foreign policy. Hans-Dietrich Genscher was Europe's longest-serving foreign minister, between 1974 and 1992, and was able to promote the policy of *détente* under both Chancellor Schmidt and Chancellor Kohl. Before him Walter Scheel of the FDP served as foreign minister assisting Brandt's *Ostpolitik*.

One of the key features of the tiny German liberal party has been its disproportionate amount of political influence and power in the FRG in comparison to its diminutive size. Although the FDP has derived great benefit from the German electoral system and has never failed to clear its 5 per cent clause at federal level, the liberal vote has fluctuated between just under 6 per cent (5.8 in 1969) and just under 13 per cent (12.8 in 1961). With hard-core electoral support (*Stammwähler*) of around only 3 or 4 per cent, the Liberals face a fresh struggle to clear the 5 per cent hurdle at each federal poll. Surmounting the 5 per cent hurdle has of course been essential to the party's survival, since it did not win a single constituency between 1957 and 1987.

Despite the inherent weakness of their position in the party system, the Free Democrats were able to hold enough parliamentary seats between 1949 and 1990 to prevent the establishment of a standard two-party system along the lines of the British or North American models. Even when some political commentators described it as a 'two-and-a-half party system' (1961–83 in West Germany), it meant that there were two dominant parties (*Volksparteien*) and one minor party, rather than a straightforward two-party or multi-party system.[10]

It was in fact precisely the nature of Germany's electoral law within the broader framework of its political system that enabled the FDP to participate in fifteen of the nineteen cabinets formed at national level between 1949 and 1998. During that same period the Liberals also spent more time in federal government than any other party, as well as providing two federal presidents, Theodor Heuss and Walter Scheel.[11]

Since the formation of the first SPD/Green federal coalition government in 1998, renewed in 2002, the FDP has again been relegated to the opposition benches in the *Bundestag*. Nevertheless, the Liberals have still never failed to clear the 5 per cent hurdle at federal level, and they are currently represented in four regional parliaments: one in partnership with the SPD and three together with the CDU. In December 2000 the membership of the FDP was just under 63,000.

7.2.4   Alliance 90/the Greens

The West German Green Party (*die Grüne Partei – die Grünen*) really was a different phenomenon from the other political parties. It developed from an environmental movement which emerged gradually, growing out of the citizens' initiative groups (*Bürgerinitiativen*) established in the late 1960s. Although there were some small 'new left' protest movements gathering at that time in the Netherlands, France and Italy, it was not until a decade later that Green parties arose in other European countries too, for example Sweden and Austria. Yet the German Green Party has proved to be the most successful one in Europe.

One explanation for the success of the German Green movement is often felt to be that it developed from the grass roots upwards, and not from the top downwards. It did not follow the usual development pattern of most political parties. Indeed, it was not a political party at all to begin with.

The Greens began by addressing the citizens' real concerns in a practical way in their local communities. Issues such as building a kindergarten, a new hospital, rest home for their elderly relatives or addressing their worries about new road schemes were frequently more important to people in their everyday lives than some distant foreign policy initiative being debated in the *Bundestag* by distant politicians, with whom they had little real contact.

The development of a new middle class in West Germany, amidst changing social structures and a revised value system of postmodernism also made a contribution to the movement as a whole. Although initially of very limited electoral appeal, the Greens originally consisted of various factions and therefore found some resonance in different groups. One strand was of course the Peace Movement (*Friedensbewegung*), which had a strong anti-nuclear element. The Greens tended anyway to establish locally in the first instance, and in 1977, for instance, they took part in local elections in Lower Saxony, following the controversial decision to build a nuclear waste disposal unit in Gorleben. As a result of this and other such actions, often by citizens' initiative groups, the local and regional Green groups were also viewed by the general public as protest movements.

A hardcore communist/socialist element also joined the Green movement in its early days, and that gave rise to some in-fighting and internal division. The women's movement also had strong links and a certain overlap with the Greens; whilst not all supporters of the women's movement were also members of the Green Party, and vice versa, some were. Above all, the movement was concerned with the protection of the environment (*Umwelt*).

Whilst the West German Greens contested the 1979 European election, the party was founded nationally at the Karlsruhe conference in January 1980. Around one thousand 'rainbow' delegates from the various factions came together to establish the Green Party (*die Grüne Partei*) at federal level. Later that year the newly established party contested the 1980 federal election, but to no avail. Firstly, it was too early for a new party, only just founded at federal level, to gain any real electoral success. Secondly, 1980 was the year of the famous 'Schmidt-Strauß battle' for the chancellorship, and the whole campaign tended to polarise the electorate. There was a lot of political mud-slinging, and voters tended to line up in one of two main camps, with only a very small minority having time for the Greens.

However the Greens did manage to clear the federal electoral system's 5 per cent hurdle at the premature federal poll in 1983; this had been brought forward after the unusual political events of October 1982 with the unplanned change in power at federal level, when Kohl became Chancellor. The Green Party was rewarded with 5.6 per cent of the second votes and 27 members of parliament in Bonn. The party increased its share of the national vote four years later, consolidating its position as a federal party. Unfortunately the

Greens did not embrace the overriding theme of German Unity in 1990, and as a consequence the Greens in western Germany just failed to satisfy the revised electoral clause, applying to the 1990 poll only. The only representation gained was from the east German Greens.

By way of reaction to this state of affairs a new all-German Green party, consisting of a merger of those in the western territories (the Greens) and those in the eastern territories (a collection of different civil rights and former GDR opposition groups known as Alliance 90) was formed in 1993, under the new name of the Alliance 90/the Greens (*Bündnis 90/ die Grünen*). Such a merger was sorely needed and has since proved advantageous for the party.

The Green movement in Germany has gone from stormy beginnings and considerable internal division between the realist and the fundamentalist wings (*Realos* versus *Fundis*), always straining to emphasise its different approach – Petra Kelly insisted 'we are the anti-party party' (*wir sind die Anti-Parteien Partei*) in 1980. The emphasis on basic democratic values *basisdemokratisch*), building up from the grassroots, freedom from violence (*gewaltfrei*) in its wider sense, including for example violence towards foreign workers in Germany, and of course respect for the environment (*umweltfreundlich*) certainly brought an unsettling aspect into the German party system. Until the arrival of the Greens on the political stage the political and party systems had been considered stable, not to say predictable in the extreme.[12]

When Alliance 90/the Greens first entered into a federal coalition government with the SPD in Bonn in 1998, and again in Berlin in 2002, the environmentalists had gone from a protest movement at local and regional level to becoming an established party. A good illustration of this is perhaps the changes in the career of their most popular and high profile politician, Joschka Fischer. Fischer, born in 1948, came to the Greens via the student movement (*Studentenbewegung*) of the 1960s; he was a member of the '68 protest movement and a supporter of militant, left-wing alternative politics. He went from being West Germany's first minister for the environment at *Land* level (in Hesse 1985–87) to becoming Germany's foreign minister, presiding, amongst other things, over some of the Iraq debates at the United Nations.

The Greens struggled at first to surmount Germany's electoral hurdle, yet they built up gradually, starting at local level first, then gained success in various regional parliaments and finally entered the *Bundestag* and national politics. At the last federal contest Alliance 90/the Greens out-polled the Liberals. At the regional elections in February 2003 they also out-polled the liberal party in both Hesse and Lower Saxony. Following those polls the Greens were, however, represented in only two federal state governments: with the

SPD in NRW and Schleswig-Holstein. The membership figure for the party was given in December 2000 as just below 47,000.

7.2.5 The PDS

The Party of Democratic Socialism (PDS) grew out of the Socialist Unity Party (SED), which was the ruling party in the former German Democratic Republic (GDR). In December 1989, just after the fall of the Berlin Wall, the party called itself the SED/PDS, under the chairmanship of Gregor Gysi. The special circumstances of the first all-German elections in 1990 introduced a special version of the electoral law, which envisaged a separate 5 per cent hurdle (or at least three constituency sets) for eastern and western Germany. This 'dispensation' for any parties competing in the eastern territories for the first time – valid only for the 1990 federal election – meant that the new party, which from February 1990 called itself simply the PDS, was granted representation in the first all-German *Bundestag*. Although the PDS gained only 2.4 per cent in Germany as a whole, it polled around 12 per cent of the vote in the east and was allocated 17 seats.

At the next federal election in 1994 it was clear that the process of German Unity was going to take some time. After the initial euphoria had subsided and the massive political, economic, social and cultural problems became apparent in the cold light of day, disenchantment set in, particularly in the east. Owing to the cultural and historical differences between the territories of what for just over 40 years had been West and East Germany, the PDS, also known as the 'political force of the left' (*die linke Kraft*), quickly became the political party representing east German interests.

Whilst many young East Germans applauded the demise of the GDR's political system and headed west, exploiting their new freedom to travel, a hard core remained, especially among the older generation of East Germans, who longed for the return of law and order, full employment, fixed prices and rents. Amongst those who stayed in the east the PDS had managed to carve out a niche for itself as a regional protest party in the new federal states, representing the interests of those disaffected with having been 'unified'.

A stark contrast exists between the membership of the PDS and those who actually vote for the party. Whilst nearly 60 per cent of PDS members are either pensioners or close to retirement and only around 5 per cent are under 30, the majority of its electoral support has often come from the younger generation. In 2002 the PDS gained the most votes from both men and women in the 30–44 age group.[13]

In 1994 the PDS, despite depleted membership,[14] increased its share of the vote, although not quite to the 5 per cent required (4.4. per cent) in the new Germany. However, the party won almost 20 per cent of the vote in the east, though only 1 per cent in the west. Even though the 5 per cent clause applied to the whole of Germany in 1994, the PDS won four constituencies (at least three is the stipulation), all in their strongholds of East Berlin. Former leaders Lothar Bisky and Gregor Gysi skilfully embraced the support of unreconstructed communists, whilst simultaneously promoting a modernised, 'new' party, which believed in following the traditions of Marx and Engels, but *not* Lenin, Stalin and Honecker.

In the federal elections of 1998 the Party of Democratic Socialism, by that time firmly established in a five-party system, succeeded in clearing the electoral system's 5 per cent hurdle for the first time (5.1 per cent), as well as winning the same four constituencies in east Berlin. In this way it qualified for parliamentary seats (35) on both counts. It remained very much an East German party, recording over 20 per cent (21.6) in the new federal states (die *neuen Bundesländer*).

The electoral performance of the PDS was crucial to the results of the 2002 contest (see 6.1). As a result of constituency boundary changes in Berlin, the 'post-communists' gained just two, not the required three, constituencies, and at the same time could not reach the magic figure of 5 per cent of the second votes (4 per cent in 2002). That of course forced the new chairperson, Gabriele (Gabi) Zimmer, and the PDS into a period of reflection and renewal. On 7 May 2003 Gabi Zimmer announced that she would not be standing again for the position of Chair (*Vorsitzende*) of the PDS. Any further changes and developments in the party of the left may also be affected by the future standing of the 'Communist Platform' faction within the party.

So the electoral system again played a key role in influencing the fate of the PDS too. Since the federal election of 2002 Germany has returned to a four-party system at federal level. It remains to be seen how far the Party of Democratic Socialism is going to succeed in regrouping and continuing to make its presence felt. The position is likely to be influenced by its performance at regional level; the PDS remains in coalition with the SPD in the *Land* Berlin and also in Mecklenburg-West Pomerania.

At the last regional poll in Mecklenburg in 2002 the PDS dropped 8 per cent of its vote, but the three-party system of SPD/CDU/PDS, with the FDP, Alliance 90/the Greens and all other parties falling below the cut-off threshold. Despite the disappointment of the 2002 federal election, the PDS is likely to remain a dominant feature in the eastern territories, where it still enjoys buoyant support as the east German 'people's party' (*die ostdeutsche Volkspartei*). The PDS has the highest membership of any party in the east. With over 79,000 members in the new states it surpasses the membership of both the SPD (just under 28,000 in the east) and the CDU (just over 56,000). However, the PDS has only just under 4,000 members in the west.[15]

7.2.6 Parties of the Far Right

The NPD When the NPD (*Nationaldemokkratische Partei Deutschlands*) was founded in 1964, it caused quite a stir in political circles; it was the first new party to be established since 1949. The party became a home for a variety of radical and nationalistic groups on the far right of the political spectrum, including some splinter groups that had been banned. The dramatic rise of the NPD coincided with the Federal Republic's first economic recession, bringing some unemployment, and, politically speaking, the generally uncertain time of the Grand Coalition federal government (1966–69).

During that three-year period the new party managed to pick up enough protest votes to clear the 5 per cent hurdle in no fewer than seven regional parliaments in West Germany (see 3.1). That included clearing the 10 per cent clause in the Bavarian *Land* elections in 1966.[16] So this was a period when serious consideration was given to changing the federal electoral law (a 10 per cent clause was mentioned). The question of applying to the Federal Constitutional Court for a ban also came up. In the end the politicians left it to the voters, and the National Democratic Party recorded 4.3 per cent of the valid second votes. The party was prevented from entering politics at federal level by the electoral system.

Although the far right party had set hearts beating faster in 1969, its share of the vote dwindled to 0.6 per cent at the next federal election in 1972. At its peak the NPD had a membership of around 30,000. Its limited support was strongest in Bavaria and Baden-Württemberg, with pockets of voters in Hessen and Lower Saxony too.

As the NPD began to fade rapidly, it formed an electoral alliance with the DVU (see below), another far right party, in 1987. At local and regional elections in Germany the NPD experiences very occasional success – for example 6.6 per cent in 1989 at the local polls in Frankfurt – but gains negligible support at federal elections. Indeed, in 2002 the NPD polled 0.4 per cent of the vote. Any party which gains less than 0.5 per cent does not have its election expenses reimbursed.

The DVU The German People's Party (*Deutsche Volksunion – DVU*) was founded in 1971, 100 years after the first German unification, by the wealthy Munich publisher Gerhard Frey, not as a political party at first, but as a way of collecting together any supporters of the far right. That included many of the members of the NPD, which was starting to disintegrate at that time.

In cooperation with the NPD Frey founded the *Deutsche Volksunion – Liste D* (the German People's Party) in March 1987. Frey even recommended his supporters to give their vote to the NPD in certain elections, as he did for example in Bavaria in 1986. Above all, he was able to offer financial support. The DVU gained seats in the Bremen state parliament in the late 1980s and 1990s (6.2 per cent in 1991), as well as in Schleswig-Holstein in 1997 (6.3 per cent in 1992).

Frey, who was always a strong proponent of restoring Germany to its 1937 borders, had the wind taken out of his sails with German Unity in 1990. Exploratory talks between Frey and the Republican leader Schönhuber (see below) regarding possible merger of their parties took place in 1994, but came to nothing. The DVU has remained a small protest party, with dwindling support from only a handful of disillusioned malcontents.

Despite this general picture, the DVU was surprisingly successful in the 1998 Sachsen-Anhalt regional election. The party's usual approach has been to target particular areas in the context of specific issues – often ones with a high percentage of foreigners residing in them – with leaflets and mail shots, usually sent out electronically from its Munich headquarters. Generally speaking, however, the German electoral system regulated the party's limited appeal by restricting access to local, regional and national parliaments.

The Republicans In 1983 Franz Schönhuber, a Bavarian journalist and popular media presenter, left the CSU following a disagreement with Franz Josef Strauß, and formed the far fight Republican Party (*die Republikaner*). Owing largely to the demagogic appeal of Schönhuber himself, who drew large crowds wherever he spoke – not just in Bavarian beer halls – the party gained a lot of publicity.

Although the Republicans had less electoral support than Le Pen's National Front and some of the other parties of the far right across Europe at the time, the media both in Germany and abroad were quick to draw parallels with Schönhuber and Hitler in terms of the content and style of his speeches, and particularly the hysterical reactions of some of his audiences.

The first big success for the party occurred when it won representation in the West Berlin election of 1989. When the party was accused of being anti-foreigner, Schönhuber countered with a piece of typical rhetoric by stating that the Republicans were not against foreigners, they were simply pro-German: *wir sind nicht ausländerfeindlich, wir sind deutschfreundlich.* The party also secured 7 per cent in the 1989 European election. Some observers were taken by surprise when the Republicans recorded over 10 per cent of the vote at the Baden-Württemberg regional elections in 1992 and entered the Stuttgart parliament again in 1996.

Since December 1994, when Schönhuber was removed as leader and replaced by Rolf Schlierer, very little has been heard of the Republicans, viewed nowadays very much as a spent force. As with other parties of the far right, the cut-off clause in German electoral politics has ensured that minority extremist views have, generally speaking, not received representation in Germany's political institutions in a manner out of proportion to their strength of support.

Notes

1   Op. cit., Patterson and Southern, p. 172.
2   Eva Kolinsky (1993), 'Das Parteiensystem in der Bundesrepublik: Forschungsthemen und Entwicklungslinien', in Oskar Niedermayer and Richard Stöss (eds), *Stand und Perspektiven der Parteienforschung in Deutschland*, Opladen.
3   Op. cit., Korte, p. 105.
4   See Peter James (1995), *The Politics of Bavaria – An Exception to the Rule*, Aldershot: Avebury, pp. 93–94.
5   Referred to in Stephen Padgett and Tony Burkett (1986), *Political Parties and Elections in West Germany*, London and New York: Hurst, p. 115.
6   For a fuller account of the incident see Peter James (1998), 'Franz Josef Strauß – Lasting Legacy or Transitory Phenomenon', *German Politics*, Vol. 7, No. 2, August, especially pp. 207–208.
7   See *der Spiegel* no. 4, 20 Janaury 2003, pp. 30/31, entitled 'Stoiber's Comeback'. Although Joschka Fischer of the Greens was still the most popular German politician and Angela Merkel (CDU) was second in the survey, Edmund Stoiber jumped to third place, with Gerhard Schröder in eighth position.
8   See David P. Conradt (2001), *The German Polity*, 7th edn, New York: Longman, p. 119.
9   See article 'British AMS versus German Personalised PR: Not So Different' by Alan Siaroff (2000) in *Representation*, Vol. 37, No. 1, Summer.
10   Gerard Braunthal (1996), *Parties and Politics in Modern Germany*, Colorado and Oxford: Westview Press, p. 78.
11   For further details see David P. Conradt, op. cit., pp. 124–6.
12   See Lewis J. Edinger (1986), *West German Politics*, New York: Columbia University Press, p. 179.
13   Bericht der Forschungsgruppe Wahlen e.V. zur Bundestgswahl 2002, p. 54.

14 The membership of the PDS fell from 284,000 in December 1990 to 150,000 in 1993 – quoted in Gerard Braunthal (1996), *Parties and Politics in Modern Germany*, New York: Westview Press, p. 156.
15 All party membership figures in this section are taken from the table on p. 121 of the article 'The German Party System – Continuity and Change' by Thomas Saalfeld (2002) in *German Politics*, Vol. 11, No. 3, December.
16 Bavaria had a 10 per cent electoral hurdle until 1973. In 1966 the NPD actually replaced the Bavarian FDP in Munich for the four-year period of legislature. The situation was reversed in 1970.

Chapter 8

The Diversity of Electoral Politics in Practice

The German federal system of 'unity in diversity' throws up a few idiosyncratic aspects of German electoral politics and electoral systems in a practical context. These are to be found in the different *Länder* that constitute Germany, given that differences, to a greater or lesser extent, exist not only between the federal states themselves, but also in some cases even between different regions within the states. By closer examination of the prevailing circumstances at *Land* level, it is possible to put some of the various aspects and influences of German electoral politics in context.

8.1 Baden-Württemberg

Baden-Württemberg is the third largest of the current 16 federal states in Germany, both in terms of population, with over ten and a half million inhabitants, including well over a million foreigners, and also in terms of territory. The new *Land* was created in 1952 by amalgamating the three *Länder* of Württemberg-Baden (capital Stuttgart), Württemberg-Hohenzollern (capital Tübingen) and Südbaden (capital Freiburg).

All three regions have their own historical and cultural traditions, so it was initially a difficult birth. In fact the original founding of the new federal state of Baden-Württemberg on 25 April 1952 was not uncontroversial amongst its inhabitants, many of who felt strongly attached to their own particular regions. For many years the lack of acceptance, especially in Baden, rumbled on, to such an extent that the Federal Constitutional Court arranged another referendum on 7 June 1970. There was an overwhelming vote in favour of accepting Germany's 'southwest state' (*Südweststaat*), with its capital Stuttgart.

For many years now Baden-Württemberg has been viewed as one of Germany's most important federal states, with a strong economy, a high GDP per head of population and an unemployment rate below the national average. These factors, and others too, including its numerous areas of outstanding natural beauty, have all contributed to the high-profile status of this *Land*.

Its economic success is based on a wide variety of successful medium-sized businesses (*Mittelstand*) and in particular some major computer-related companies, as well as the automobile industry with such car giants as Daimler-Chrysler (Mercedes-Benz), Porsche and Audi. It also has some idiosyncratic features in its political system, including the most complex electoral system of all the federal states.

Voters at local elections in Baden-Württemberg have the practices of *kumulieren* and *panaschieren* available to them. The voter is given the same number of votes as there are deputies to elect, and is allowed to 'accumulate' up to three votes for one candidate. This process in known in German as *kumulieren*, whereby one, two, or three votes can be given to a candidate, if the voter so wishes. The process of *panaschieren* means that voters may elect candidates from different parties – they are not restricted to the candidates of just one party. Such procedures offer the individual voter greater choice to select the candidates he or she feels will represent them best, without the constraints of being limited to just one political party.

At regional elections for the Stuttgart parliament seventy deputies are selected directly with the first vote in single constituencies. The remaining fifty representatives of the *Landtag*, which contains a total of 120 members of parliament, are elected on the basis of the proportional results of the parties, as demonstrated by the best of the seventy constituency candidates. Unusually, there are no party lists in Baden-Württemberg at a *Landtagswahl*, so it is in fact the only one of the 16 federal states which has constituency candidates only at a regional election. That makes it difficult for the parties to plan, and it also means that additional mandates (*Überhangmandate*) can often occur. If they do, the other parties are given mandates to balance out the situation (*Ausgleichsmandate*). Such a procedure can of course easily increase the size of the regional parliament. In 1996, for example, it grew to 155, instead of the envisaged 120![1]

In terms of religious denomination, there is an approximately equal split between Catholics and Protestants in Germany's 'southwest state'. The *Südweststaat* has been governed by a CDU minister president since 1953, sometimes with SPD and FDP support. Nevertheless, several parties have had some political success from time to time, although in recent years the CDU has continued to dominate, with *Ministerpräsident* Erwin Teufel (CDU) sometimes governing alone and sometimes leading coalitions with the FDP/DVP, as has been the case since the regional elections of 2001. Teufel has headed the state government since 1991.

Baden-Württemberg is a state with a particularly large share of non-Germans living in it – over 1.3 million out of a population of some 10.6 million. This may go some way towards explaining why the right-wing extremist Republican Party (*die Republikaner*) entered the Stuttgart parliament after both the 1992 and 1996 state elections, although the party narrowly failed to clear the 5 per cent hurdle at the last regional poll. This was also the federal state where the Green Party first entered a regional parliament in 1979/80 and the Greens have enjoyed relatively strong support ever since.

Since the *Land* was created three years after the 1949 *Grundgesetz*, the Baden-Württemberg constitution of 11 November 1953 drew heavily on the West German constitution, almost certainly benefiting from that. A general feeling would appear to exist that, on the whole, the constitution has served the federal state and its people well, with relatively few amendments proving necessary. It provides for the use of direct democracy via device of the referendum.

Paradoxically, all the main parties gain support here, although the CDU has dominated the party system. This, despite what should be, and often is, a relatively favourable social structure for the SPD, in terms of its share of Protestants and manual workers. Baden-Württemberg is also known as 'the home territory of liberalism' (*Stammland/Musterländle der Liberalen*), and is an area in which the Greens, and even the Republicans (see above) have had some success. After the liberal politician Reinhard Maier, the state's first minister president, had headed a coalition government of FDP/DVP, SPD, and GB/BHE against the CDU, the Christian Democrats then took over the reigns of power under Gebhard Müller, Kurt Georg Kiesinger, Hans Filbinger, Lothar Späth and now Erwin Teufel. Between 1972 and 1992 the CDU was able to rule in Stuttgart with an absolute majority. From 1992 until 1996 a Grand Coalition was in charge and currently there is a CDU/FDP coalition government.

At local level too there is plenty of room for the citizens to participate in the political process. The people elect their local mayor directly; he remains in post for eight years, which creates a three-year overlap with the five-year period of the town councils. Half of the mayors are independents, with no party political ties.

8.2 Bavaria

In terms of population, Bavaria is the second largest (over 12 million inhabitants) of the 16 federal states, after North-Rhine Westphalia, although

Bavaria is geographically the largest *Land* (it occupies the almost 20 per cent of the territory of the FRG). Although the Free State of Bavaria (*der Freistaat Bayern*), with its idiosyncratic features and special history and traditions, is often viewed as an exception to the rule in the Federal Republic (*in Bayern gehen die Uhren anders*), there is considerable diversity in the other federal states too. Bavaria's southern neighbour, BadenWürttemberg (see above) also has its own political idiosyncrasies, and indeed shares some special features with it.

So the talk of Bavarian independence (*bayerische Eigenständigkeit*) should not detract from this illustration of the political and electoral considerations that are relevant to each *Land* in the Federal Republic. Remember that the German federal system thrives on the system of unity in diversity (*Einheit in Vielfalt*). The FRG is of course a single unit, which nevertheless contains considerable variety within its overall structure. It is also a developing culture in a country where things do not stand still, and one where participatory federalism (*Beteiligungsföderalismus*) plays a crucial role.

In the early postwar years Bavaria had a unique electoral system amongst the federal states of the FRG. It was the only *Land* which had a 10 per cent clause for its regional elections. All the other states had a 5 per cent clause. Until 1973 a party had to gain at least 10 per cent of the vote in any one of the seven governmental districts (*Regierungsbezirke*) in Bavaria in order to enter the Bavarian *Landtag* in Munich. There were, and still are, one or two special features of the Bavarian political system which means that in practice the Free State of Bavaria has been able to adopt a special position (*Sonderstellung*) in the Federal Republic.

Baden Württemberg and Bavaria are just two examples of German federal states that display some variety within the *Land*, in terms of both history and tradition and political factors such as voting patterns. As far as Bavaria is concerned, the four lines of descent of its inhabitants (Bavarians, Franconians, Swabians and Germans from the Sudetenland) represent very significant but different traditions. Election results have sometimes followed a slightly different course in each of the seven governmental districts of Upper, Central and Lower Franconia, Upper and Lower Bavaria and Bavarian Swabia.

Regional elections in Bavaria were traditionally held every four years, and the timing of them in recent years meant that they occurred only weeks before federal elections. It is interesting to see that German voters often behave differently in different electoral contexts. The differences in the way in which voters behave at federal and regional polls (true for most federal states) was emphasised again in September 1994. The same Bavarian voters displayed slightly different electoral behaviour – especially with regard to the FDP, which usually performs badly in Bavaria, compared with the way in which they cast their votes just two weeks later at the federal poll. The votes cast for the CSU, SPD and FDP at the Bavarian regional election were 52.8, 30.1, and 2.8 per cent respectively, whilst at the federal election fourteen days later the votes cast for those same parties were 51.2, 29.6, and 6.4 per cent respectively. Since regional elections in Bavaria now take place every five years, starting with the September 2003 poll, the situation has changed, as far as the proximity of Bavarian and federal polls are concerned.

Local elections in Bavaria, just as in Baden Württemberg (see above), allow the voters to avail themselves of the practices of *kumulieren* (giving one, two or three votes to one candidate) and *panaschieren* (giving votes to candidates on different party lists), if they so wish. Research in both states reveals that voters at local elections (*Kommunalwahlen*) do in fact often take advantage of this facility. The voter has as many votes at his/her disposal as there are candidates. The ballot paper at a Bavarian local election is often the size of a daily newspaper, since it contains the names of every candidate of every party.

The Bavarian second chamber (*der Senat*) was a unique feature amongst the German *Länder*, until its abolition on 31 December 1999. A special electoral process was used to select the 60 members of Bavaria's postwar second chamber. Members, who had to be at least 40 years old and were elected for six years, came from agriculture and forestry, the trade unions, the communes and local interest groups, industry and commerce, the craft trades, the cooperatives, the religious orders, the welfare organisations, the free professions and the universities and academies.

It was decided in 1946 to establish a Bavarian *Senat* (literally, a council of elders) as one of the four highest organs of state, along with the *Landtag*, the state government and the Bavarian Constitutional Court (article 64 of the Bavarian constitution). Despite the fact that the Bavarian second chamber now no longer exists, it did add an extra dimension to electoral politics in Bavaria for over 40 years. On 8 February 1998 three referenda were held in Bavaria, which introduced the most far-reaching changes in the Bavarian constitution since 1946, including the abolition of the second chamber. The *Landtag* in Munich, the Maximilianeum, now contains 180, instead of the usual 204 deputies, following the most recent Bavarian *Landtagswahl* of September 2003.

A unique aspect of the Bavarian party system is that it has been dominated by a unique party, the CSU. The CSU is the only political party in Germany that is at the same time both a regional and a federal party, since it always forms a joint parliamentary party (*Fraktion*) with the CDU. With the exception of 1954–57 every postwar Bavarian government has contained the CSU; the party has dominated Bavarian politics more than any other party in any other area of Germany. Under the leadership of Bavarian minister presidents Alfons Goppel and Franz Josef Strauß in particular the CSU became *the* Bavarian party of state *par excellence*.

8.3 Berlin

Berlin of course occupies a very special position in German history. It is now both Germany's capital city again, with a current population of around three and a half million, as well as being one of the Federal Republic's sixteen *Länder*. It has been known since 1949 as one of Germany's three 'city states' (*Stadtstaaten*), the others being Bremen and Hamburg. Berlin is often referred to as a metropolis (*Metropole*) or city of world significance (*Weltstadt*), and it has a fascinating history, in some ways reflecting the history of Germany itself. The city's origins can be traced back to 1237 and 1244, with the growth of two towns on the river Spree, Berlin and Cölln.[2]

After becoming the capital of a unified Germany in 1871, Berlin was home to the Reichstag, which housed the German government of the day and first introduced a secret ballot and equal voting rights. Even at the end of the nineteenth century people spoke of 'red Berlin' (*das rote Berlin*), referring to the dominance of the SPD (and the USPD). The city has traditionally been associated with the German workers' movement with a history of opposition to communism; in fact the SPD was often considered to be the 'Berlinpartei'. Under West Germany Ernst Reuter and Willy Brandt were two charismatic mayors (*Regierende Bürgermeister* of Berlin. Today, Berlin's town hall is still known as '*das rote Rathaus*'. After the Wall was built in 1961, Berlin developed even greater symbolic significance, in terms of representing a divided city in a divided nation; the East German government, under Soviet influence, underlined this state of affairs by declaring East Berlin to be the capital of the GDR (*Hauptstadt der DDR*).

In May 1996 referenda were held regarding a fusion of the *Länder* of Berlin and Brandenburg, but the 'merger' did not happen. In Berlin there was a small majority in favour of the merger, but in Brandenburg there was a sizeable majority against. A closer look at the vote reveals that in fact a majority of West Berliners voted *for* the merger, but in East Berlin the majority was *against*.[3]

After German Unity Berlin became known as 'Europe's biggest building site', as most of the governmental institutions moved from Bonn to Berlin. The significance of Berlin again becoming the capital of the New Germany, created on 3 October 1990, and also of the *Bundestag* returning to the *Reichstagsgebäude* in Berlin in 1999, cannot be underestimated. Just as in other *Länder* too, Berlin could certainly be considered to be a special case, not only because of its symbolic significance and special place in German history, but also because of its special status after 1949. Although West Berlin, geographically speaking, was an 'island' in the territory of the GDR, the attempt was made to include it legally, politically and economically, as far as possible, in the basic structures of the FRG.

As a result of the four-power agreement of the Allies after the Second World War, the 22 Berlin parliamentary deputies could not be directly elected; they were sent to the West Berlin parliament (*Abgeordnetenhaus*) and the federal parliament (*Bundestag*) in Bonn, according to the relative strengths of the parties in West Germany. In the final counting of the votes on federal laws and in the election of the Federal President, the votes of the Berlin deputies could not be included, even though the actual election of the Federal President of the FRG often took place in West Berlin.

The legislative body in Berlin is known as the House of Deputies (*Abgeordnetenhaus*). According to the Berlin constitution this houses the people's representatives chosen by those eligible to vote (*die Volksvertretung*); it consists of 150 elected deputies. The first free postwar elections were held on 20 October 1946 in West Berlin. On that occasion there was an amazing 92.3 per cent turnout in the whole of Berlin, and at the elections in West Berlin in 1958 the figure was 92.9 per cent. In Berlin the government is known as the senate (*der Senat*). The Berlin constitution deliberately did not follow the 'chancellor principle', which obtains at federal level in Germany, with the result that the House of Deputies can force the Senate, and/or individual members of it to resign via a vote of no confidence. The ruling mayor, together with the Senate, determines policy guidelines (*Richtlinien*).

On 2 December 1990, the date of the all-German elections, following German Unity two months earlier, a parliament representing the whole of Berlin was chosen again for the first time since October 1946. The 5 per cent electoral clause was valid separately for the territory of both East and West Berlin, and the Hare/Niemeyer system of allocating votes, rather than the d'Hondt method was introduced (see 2.7). Any additional mandates (*Überhangmandate*) that occur are balanced out via *Ausgleichmandate* (see 2.5). That can of course sometimes mean an increase in the number of Berlin deputies. Sixty per cent of the mandates have usually been chosen via the constituencies, as direct seats, with the remainder coming from the party lists. For local elections in Berlin a voting system of pure proportional representation is used, and in 1999 a 3 per cent clause cut-off clause was introduced for the first time.

Since 1990 eligible voters in Berlin have been able to participate directly in both federal German and European elections. Following a Grand Coalition between the two major parties in 1999 under minister president Diepgen (CDU), a new political constellation took over the government of the famous city state. At the time of writing (2003) Berlin is one of only two German federal states which has an SPD/PDS coalition government, presided over by Klaus Wowereit (SPD). The other *Land* with an SPD/PDS ('red-red') government is Mecklenburg-West Pomerania.

The post-1945 political history of Berlin is full of remarkable events. The Soviet Military Administration in Germany (SMAD) insisted on the forced marriage of the SPD and KPD to form the SED in April 1946. It also created an *'Einheitsfront'* of so-called 'anti-fascist democratic parties', with new creations such as the farmers and peasants party (*Bauernpartei*) and the national democratic party (*Nationaldemokratische Partei*), as part of a united list of parties (*Einheitsliste*) presented to the voters in east Berlin under the regime of the GDR between 1949 and 1990.

Berlin has been termed an international capital of repute and a metropolis, but it is in no way an economic metropolis (*keine Wirtschaftsmetropole*).[4] In terms of its economy, it still has structural and financial problems to overcome, but there is confidence amongst its inhabitants that Berlin, supported by its amazing number of cultural institutions, might one day return to its glory days of the 1920s and early 1930s.

8.4 Brandenburg

The federal state of Brandenburg has the most expansive territory of the new states (*die neuen Länder*) in the east. Brandenburg can look back on more than one thousand years of history, which can be traced back to its first ruling tribe, the Ascaniens (1134–1320). Although its territory is expansive and in fact encircles Berlin completely, Brandenburg has only 2.6 million inhabitants. It has the lowest population density of any of the 16 federal states. As with all the new *Länder*, Brandenburg found the sudden change from a centrally planned economy under the socialist system in the GDR to the capitalist market economy in the FRG and integration into the European

Union difficult. Nevertheless, unemployment in Brandenburg is amongst the lowest in the east.

Following the state organisational law of 1 November 1990, Brandenburg's own constitution came into force on 21 August 1992, after a referendum in June of that year. It permits, amongst other things, the regional parliament to dissolve its membership, if there is a two-thirds majority in favour of doing so. The first government in Brandenburg after German Unity was under Manfred Stolpe (SPD), and it consisted of a coalition between the SPD, the FDP and Alliance 90. In 1994 Stolpe and the SPD gained an absolute majority, although the government contained two independents in ministerial positions.

After the 1999 regional election, Stolpe led a SPD/CDU Grand Coalition government in Potsdam, with Jörg Schönbohm (CDU) as his deputy and interior minister. Stolpe retired on 26 June 2002, when Matthias Platzeck (SPD) took over as minister president. The party with the largest membership in Brandenburg is the PDS, which is the case in the eastern territories generally. Brandenburg's regional parliament normally consists of 88 deputies, with 44 selected from single-member constituencies and another 44 selected from the party lists according to PR. There are fixed lists and the seats are allocated according to the Hare/Niemeyer method. Additional mandates are permitted, but there is an upper limit – 110 – on the number of seats in the Potsdam *Landtag*. Each voter has two votes and any party wishing to enter the regional parliament must either gain 5 per cent of the valid second votes or else win one constituency. However, the 5 per cent hurdle does not apply to any political group representing the Sorbs, who's right to protect and cultivate their national identity are guaranteed by the constitution.

Direct democracy is strong in Brandenburg, promoted by the use of the plebiscite and the referendum (*Volksinitiative, Volksbegehren, Volksentscheid*), and it is the *Land* with the lowest quotas required to initiate these procedures. The SPD (see above) has dominated the political arena in the state since 1990, increasing its share of the vote from 32.9 per cent at the 1990 federal election to over 45 per cent at the *Bundestagswahl* in 1994 and 43.5 per cent at the 1998 BTW. The PDS frequently challenges the CDU nowadays, but there were serious problems for the Greens when Alliance 90 from the east joined the western Greens in 1993. It caused much internal strife and led to some resignations. Another party with serious problems in this federal state is the liberal party. At the last six elections (local, regional and federal) the Greens have failed to clear the electoral hurdle and the same applies to the FDP at the last five contests. At the regional poll in 1999 Alliance 90/the Greens recorded only 1.94 per cent, and the FDP just 1.86 per cent.

Local elections in Brandenburg are held every five years, the voter has up to three votes, and the mayors remain in office for eight years. As we saw in 8.3 above, at the proposed Berlin-Brandenburg fusion, nearly 815,000 citizens of Brandenburg, out of almost 1.3 million who voted, cast their votes against the two states joining forces. That came as a surprise to the politicians, because all the main parties, with the exception of the PDS, were in favour of the 'merger'.

8.5   Bremen

The Free Hanseatic City of Bremen (*die Freie Hansestadt Bremen*) is the smallest of the German federal states. It has less than 700,000 inhabitants and consists of the two cities, Bremen and Bremerhaven, which are separated by approximately 60km, or 40 miles, of territory belonging to Lower Saxony, connected by the river Weser. The government of the federal state of Bremen is officially known as 'the Senate of the Free Hanseatic City of Bremen' (*Senat der Freien Hansestadt Bremen*) and the parliament (the *Landtag*) is called the *Bremische Bürgerschaft*. It consists of 100 deputies: eighty for Bremen and twenty for Bremerhaven. The parliament (*Bürgerschaft*) chooses the members of the government (*Senat*), who then choose, in a secret election, from amongst their own number, two mayors. One of these mayors acts as president of the Senate – a sort of minister president.

Some of the inhabitants are happy to argue that Bremen is a special case amongst the *Länder* of the Federal Republic, since it has a long history of battling for its independence. Ever since Bremen, a small settlement on the banks of the river Weser, was elevated to the status of a bishopric in the year 787 under Charlemagne, it continued to develop, gaining city status in 1186 and joining the Hanseatic trade association in 1358.

The revolution of 1848 brought to Bremen, amongst other things, an electoral law that divided the electorate into eight classes. In 1854 an unusual constitution was introduced which guaranteed a conservative majority in the government. It was an intentionally complicated procedure which gave the Senate great power. Its members were elected for life. Things changed only when, at the end of the First World War, the sailors' revolt which started in Kiel, reached Bremen. The workers and soldiers took over power, establishing a 'socialist republic' in Bremen (*Räterepublik*) on 10 January 1919. In May 1920 a democratic parliament was finally introduced, consisting of 120 members, based on universal and equal voting rights.

In the post-1945 situation, the US occupation forces put the former social democrat Wilhelm Kaisen in charge of a government in April 1946, which contained social democrats, communists, and liberals. On 21 January 1947 the federal state of Bremen was founded; it consisted of Bremen, Bremerhaven and Wesermünde. The last two were united on 7 February 1947. A lot of emphasis was placed on basic human rights in the new constitution. The SPD was soon established as the dominant political force. Kaisen and the SPD often ruled with other parties as coalition partners, even though they had an absolute majority of the seats. The SPD has dominated the Bremen political scene, with only a few slight interruptions from occasional strong performances from other parties.

At a time of economic problems in the mid-Sixties, Bremen was one of several states where the neo-nazi NPD entered parliament (1967). Bremen also became one of the centres of the environmentalist and anti-nuclear movement. In 1979 the BGL (Bremen Green List) party was one of the first to enter a state parliament. The labour protest group (*Arbeit für Bremen/Bremerhaven*) in 1995 forced the SPD (it was a break-away group) to enter a government coalition with the CDU. The AFB disappeared again in 1999, which marked the beginning of a SPD/CDU coalition government, with Henning Scherf (SPD) as president of the senate. The far-right DVU gained representation in 1991 (having had one seat as the Liste D in 1987). Regional elections are held every four years, the last one being in May 2003. The 5 per cent clause applies separately to Bremen and Bremerhaven.

8.6 Hamburg

Bremen's close neighbour, the federal state of Hamburg – official name: the free and Hanseatic state of Hamburg (*Freie und Hansestadt Hamburg*) is also a city state. The city of Hamburg, with just over 1.7 million inhabitants, over 15 per cent of whom are foreigners, is Germany's second largest city, and at the same time of course the *Stadtstaat* of Hamburg is one of the 16 German *Länder*. Also like Bremen, Hamburg developed via shipping into one of the most important economic centres in Europe. Founded in the early ninth century, originally known as Hammaburg, it was the twelfth century when Hamburg began to take off as a port and centre of the brewing industry.

In economic terms Hamburg was always far ahead of its political development. It had the first and therefore oldest Stock Exchange in Germany in 1558, and the first Chamber of Commerce in Germany, established in 1665.

As shipbuilding declined, Hamburg nevertheless remained Germany's main seaport and most important overseas trade centre. Numerous companies from China, Japan and Taiwan have offices in the Hanseatic city, and over 3,000 firms are involved in the import/export business there. Economic success has gone from strength to strength, and today Hamburg is one of the richest and most prosperous cities in Germany, and also in Europe.

As far as the political system is concerned, it was however not until 1921 that Hamburg received its first democratic constitution. The present-day parliament is called the *Bürgerschaft* and it consists of 121 seats, with no additional mandates possible, and is elected every four years according to PR with the d'Hondt method of seat allocation. The government is known as the *Senat*, consisting of a first and second mayor and around eight to ten senators. The first mayor (*Bürgermeister*) is the President of the Senate, the equivalent of the minister president in most other federal states. Hamburg consists of seven political districts (*Bezirke*) and is divided into 104 administrative areas (*Stadtteile*).

After dominating *Land* politics for decades, the SPD was amazingly relegated to the opposition benches at the last regional election for only the second time in its postwar history. The Social Democrats were still the largest party at the *Landtagswahl* on 23 September 2001, but a somewhat unusual coalition government was formed by the CDU, FDP (with just 5.1 per cent) and Ronald Schill's *Partei der Rechtsstaatlichen Offensive*. This new far-right party was founded in 2000 by former judge Schill, known as 'Judge Merciless' (*Richter Gnadenlos*), owing to some very heavy sentences for relatively minor offences. The party is often referred to as the *Schillpartei*. It gained over 19 per cent of the vote on a 'law and order' ticket in 2001, promising to eradicate Hamburg's drug and crime problems. In this way Ole von Beust (CDU) managed to put together an 'anti-SPD' coalition (CDU, Schill party, FDP) and became the president of the Hamburg senate, that is the head of the state government. Consequently the SPD currently finds itself in opposition in the Hamburg parliament for the first time since the 'Hamburger Block' was formed against it in 1953 (by the CDU, FDP, and DP).

8.7 Hessen

The federal state of Hessen, or Hesse, was once joined together with Thuringia (*Thüringen*), and shared the same coat of arms. When the two territories were separated in 1247, they each retained the lion as its symbol. The area has a long history, stretching back to Roman times, and was first mentioned in a letter from Pope Gregory III to the cleric Bonifatius in the year 738 as 'populus Hassiorum (the people of Hessen).[5] Hessen experienced a stormy and eventful history, strongly influenced by the Peace of Westphalia at the end of the Thirty Years' War and the French Revolution, affecting territory and religion. The areas of Hessen-Kassel, Hessen-Darmstadt, the imperial city (*Reichstadt*) of Frankfurt and the Grand Duchy of Hessen and the Rhine all gained or lost territory. The democratic revolution of 1848/49, centred on the Paulskirche in Frankfurt, although it failed to establish the first German nation state, was of course a famous step. Many years later, on 19 September 1945, Ludwig Bergsträsser administered the provisional government in Darmstadt, Kassel and Wiesbaden. After Lucius D. Clay, the US military governor, had proclaimed the new Hessen, General Eisenhower, whose ancestors came from the Odenwald region of Hessen, officially announced the establishment of 'Greater Hesse', which became the present-day federal state of Hessen. The first elections for a constitutional body in Hessen (*Verfassunggebende Landesversammlung*) took place on 30 June 1946. The SPD was the largest party and that marked the beginning of three decades of dominance by the Social Democrats.

Even though the American occupation forces originally put the spotlight on the city of Frankfurt am Main by placing the first legislative bodies in the IG-Farben building there, nearby Wiesbaden, which had suffered far less war damage, was chosen as Hessen's state capital. Frankfurt soon began to dominate economic life in Hessen, as a business and banking centre. This is a federal state which is also well known for the chemical industry (for example Hoechst), electrical goods and machine tools. Hessen, along with the two most southern German states, has in recent years traditionally been an area of relatively low unemployment and high GDP.

Following the establishment of the FRG in 1949, the SPD achieved an absolute majority of the parliamentary seats at the 1950 regional elections in Hessen, and Georg August Zinn became minister president. There was a *Hessen vorn* campaign (Hessen to the fore) and leading political personalities such as Ernst Schütte, Heinrich Hemsath and Hildegard Hamm-Brücher pushed the Hessen cause forward.

In 1982 the Green Party gained 8 per cent of the vote and entered the Hessen *Landtag*. The party formed the first red-green coalition government at regional level and provided the first environment minister an any federal state (Joschka Fischer). From 1987 until 1991 a CDU-FDP government took over in Hessen, but the SPD/Green coalition under Hans Eichel soon returned. Just a few months after the first success of a red/green coalition at federal level (1998) the SPD-led regional government in Hessen was replaced at the first *Landtagswahl* since the *Bundestagswahl* by a CDU/FDP coalition.

The same thing happened again four years later. This time, however, the CDU gained an absolute majority of the seats in the Hessen parliament at the last regional contest on 2 February 2003; therefore the Christian Democrats no longer require the services of a coalition partner and they now governs alone under minister president Roland Koch. The CDU in fact gained almost 49 per cent of the vote, giving them 48 per cent of the parliamentary seats in the *Landtag* in Wiesbaden. The SPD attracted one of its worst-ever results, with less than 30 per cent of the votes. Alliance 90/the Greens cleared the 10 per cent mark and the Liberals in Hessen took almost 8 per cent.

At regional elections in Hessen, held every four years, each voter has two votes, in order to elect 55 candidates from constituencies and an equal number from the fixed party lists on a PR system, with parliamentary seats allocated according to the d'Hondt process. At local polls, also held every four years, each voter has one vote. Local mayors are chosen directly for a period of six years. They require an absolute majority in the first round.

8.8 Lower Saxony

Lower Saxony (*Niedersachsen*) is, in terms of geographical area, the second largest, after Bavaria, of the German federal states. It occupies over 13 per cent of Germany's territory. In terms of population, it is the fourth biggest, with nearly eight million inhabitants, and belongs to the 'big four'. Bavaria, Baden-Württemberg, Lower Saxony and North-Rhine Westphalia have six votes each in the *Bundesrat*, the second chamber of the German parliament.

Some of the most fertile, arable soil in the Federal Republic is to be found in this state, and agriculture and farming have always played an important part in its economy. So too however have the automobile industry, with the Volkswagen headquarters in Wolfsburg, shipbuilding, steel, chemicals and, more recently computer-related and electronics industries. With just 6 per cent of non-Germans in the population of this *Land*, that is well below average for Germany. Unemployment has sometimes been above the German average, but the state went through a structural change (see above) from a predominantly agricultural to an industrial *Land*. By 1996/97 less than 5 per cent of the inhabitants were employed in the agricultural sector, and nearly a third were in industry and the vast majority (64 per cent) were employed in the services sector.[6]

In the period 1945/46 the state of Lower Saxony was formed from territory that was, in the main, areas which had traditionally belonged to the Saxons and the Friesians. The British occupation forces first of all re-established the former states of Brunswick (Braunschweig), Oldenburg and Schaumburg-Lippe. Hanover joined soon afterwards. In the early post-war period stringent efforts were made to encourage a feeling of belonging to the newly created federal state, with its heterogeneous structure.

In the early years of the Federal Republic a multiparty system seemed to be developing in NS (*Niedersachsen*). In 1951 there were nine political parties in the *Landtag*; in 1958 a 5 per cent hurdle was introduced. NS was also a region where right-wing extremist parties, especially the SRP (*Sozialistische Reichspartei*) – it had gained 16 deputies at one point – and the BHE refugees party collected some support. However, as far as electoral trends are concerned, the federal state of NS can be split into four areas. The first of these is the thinly populated agricultural region in the northwest of the *Land*, the part covering the Lüneburg Heath between the rivers Elbe and Aller/Weser. This was always a CDU stronghold, as well as an area where the far-right picked up some votes. The Greens also gained some electoral support here (especially in university towns), owing to the proximity of Gorleben, with its nuclear waste recycling plant.

The second region is East Friesland, predominantly Protestant and a mixture of agricultural and industrial development. It includes the northern part of Oldenburg and experienced some high unemployment, as a result of the decline of shipbuilding, and is an area containing some SPD strongholds. The third region of Emsland and southern Oldenburg are Catholic areas which were formerly ruled by the bishops of Osnabrück and Münster. This is of course an area of very strong CDU support – it was a part of Germany where the CDU's predecessor, the Centre Party (*Zentrum*), traditionally gained clear majorities, and the Christian Democrats have sometimes attained up to sixty or even 70 per cent of the vote.

The fourth region of Lower Saxony is the southeastern corner that encompasses the industrial areas of Brunswick, Wolfsburg, Salzgitter and Hanover, plus the southern tip of the Harz region. This is mainly SPD territory – with the exception of the Catholic area of Eichsfeld, although more recently electoral support has fluctuated at times between the two main parties.

Until the most recent regional election in 2003, the SPD has tended to dominate the political stage – with the brief exception of a DP government under minister president Heinrich Hellwege 1955–59. In 1976 the CDU surprised many people by getting their candidate Ernst Albrecht in place as the *Landesvater* of the state. Until 1990 the Christian Democrats ruled, partly alone and partly with the Free Democrats. After Gerhard Schröder, who comes from Hanover, became Federal Chancellor in 1998, Gerhard Glogowski took over as minister president of Lower Saxony, followed by Sigmar Gabriel, both from the SPD.

On 2 February 2003, however, the same day as the *Landtagswahl* in Hessen (see above) German Social Democrat politicians were in for a great shock, when the CDU gained an absolute majority at the regional election, ejecting the ruling SPD from power in Lower Saxony, only four months after their narrow federal victory. The CDU polled 48.3 per cent of the vote, with the SPD managing a mere third of the vote (33.4 per cent), and Alliance 90/the Greens and the FDP both cleared the 5 per cent hurdle with 7.6 and 8.1 per cent respectively. It really was a tremendous political shock and an extremely grim day for the Social Democrats in Lower Saxony.

8.9 Mecklenburg-Western Pomerania

Mecklenburg-Western Pomerania (Mecklenburg-Vorpommern), one of the so-called new federal states, i.e. one of the eastern states, is in fact geographically speaking the sixth largest (in terms of area occupied), but the fourth smallest (in terms of its population), with only 1.8 million inhabitants. It is a *Land* whose development has been strongly influenced by the sea – the Baltic. There are over sixty little islands – some of them tiny – off its coast, the largest of which is Rügen. Mecklenburg-West Pomerania was first established by the Soviet military administration in June 1945, but lost the title West Pomerania (Vorpommern) from its name, with the end of the state of Prussia in February 1947. Then, as with the other East German states, it was dissolved by the GDR authorities in 1952, and finally re-established in 1990 as one of the 16 federal states of the new Germany.

The history of Mecklenburg stretches back to the year 995; its people looked back with pride on their Slavonic roots. West Pomerania belonged to Sweden for 200 years during the seventeenth century. So, as with so many of the German *Länder*, 'Meck-Pom', as it is sometimes known in Germany, is sometimes seen by its inhabitants as a special case. With its present-day capital of Schwerin, Mecklenburg (-Vorpommern) is a federal state where shipbuilding (now of course in decline), associated with the port of Rostock, and agriculture has often played an important role. As with other eastern states, Mecklenburg has suffered from very high unemployment since joining the new Germany in 1990 (17.7 per cent in June 2002, but the figure has sometimes surpassed 20 per cent). In the period 1989/90 young people left Mecklenburg in droves, looking for work and a brighter future in the west, which meant that the state remained near the bottom of the table, in socioeconomic terms.[7]

Following the first regional elections of 14 October 1990, at which the CDU (over 38 per cent) predictably outvoted the SPD (27 per cent), a CDU-FDP coalition government was formed. At the next regional election, on 16 October 1994, the CDU (37.3 per cent) and the SPD (29.5 per cent) formed a Grand Coalition in Schwerin, with the PDS as the only opposition party in the Mecklenburg parliament, as both the FDP and the Greens fell at the 5 per cent hurdle. In fact the liberal and green parties have only a few hundred members together in this federal state, and have had little success amongst the voters.

At the 1998 *Landtagswahl* the SPD out-polled the CDU for the first time in Mecklenburg, the PDS gained over 24 per cent of the vote and the first SPD-PDS coalition government in the FRG was formed, under minister president Harald Ringstorff. On 27 September 1998 the FDP and Alliance 90/the Greens both performed badly again, as the three-party system (CDU, SPD, PDS) had become firmly established in the east. It is important to remember that the six eastern *Länder* play a significant part in German election nowadays, given that just over 22 per cent (13.6 million Germans eligible to vote in 2002)[8] live there.

At the last regional poll in Mecklenburg, held on the same day as the 2002 federal election, the percentage results were as follows: SPD – 40.6, CDU – 31.4, PDS – 16.4, FDP – 4.7, Alliance 90/the Greens – 2.6, NPD – 0.8. As a consequence the SPD-PDS coalition government under Ringstorff continued in Schwerin, even though neither of the parties had really been able to fulfil its promises on policy. The post-Communist party lost 8 per cent of its vote from 1998, but the Social Democrats in Mecklenburg were able to increase their share of the vote, mainly by deriving benefit from the federal SPD's popularity. During the regional campaign the main thing the two ruling coalition partners found to agree upon was that neither wanted to work with the CDU.

Mecklenburg-Western Pomerania introduced a gentle reform of its communes (*Gemeinden*) in 1994, which abolished some of the tiny administrative units, by forming 12 new rural districts (*Landkreise*) from the former 31. The move was controversial at the time, and at the local elections in 1994 no mayors, lord mayors or *Landräte* were elected, although five years later honorary mayors were directly chosen for a period of between seven and nine years. The voter has up to three votes in a local election. In a regional election, to elect the 71 deputies, the voter has two votes, since there is an almost equal number of constituency and list votes.

The constitution of 23 May 1993 was not Meck-Pom's first democratic one. In 1919 and 1920 the two free states of Mecklenburg and Pomerania (the Prussian constitution was valid for Pomerania from 1920 onwards) set out constitutional arrangements, and in 1989/90 the *Land* brought in articles dealing with basic rights such as, in article three: 'parties and citizens' movements play a part in the formation of the political will of the people'.

8.10 North-Rhine Westphalia

North-Rhine Westphalia (*Nordrhein-Westfalen*) is Germany's most densely populated *Land* (with 528 people per square km), and the one with the largest number of inhabitants – over 18 million. It was a postwar artificial creation (*Retortenland*), mainly from former Prussian territory, when it was created in 1946 under a British military government. NRW is a federal state with a long history of immigration from various countries. Many foreigners, from Poland especially, came to work in the Ruhr industrial area, associated for many years with coal-mining and steel. Numerous foreign workers (*Gastarbeiter*) arrived there in the 1950s and 1960s too, and NRW still has an above average number of foreign workers, especially in big cities such as Cologne, Düsseldorf and Duisburg, where the percentage of non-Germans reaches around 20 per cent of the population. There are 30 *Großstädte* (big towns/cities with a population of 100,00).

The German inhabitants are a heterogeneous mix, in terms of socioeconomic and denominational factors, as well as subcultures. The Rhineland is a predominantly Catholic area, but there is also a sizeable Protestant population, which partly explains why the state has sometimes been run by the CDU and sometimes the SPD. In political terms this has always been a federal state of some significance for three reasons. Firstly because of its large population, secondly the economic significance of the *Ruhrgebiet* for many years in the former West Germany, and thirdly the closeness of Düsseldorf, the state capital, to Bonn, the former capital and seat of government. In regional polls each voter has only one vote to select the 151 constituency candidates and the 50 list deputies who enter the *Landtag*. The Free Democrats have sometimes formed government coalitions in NRW with either of the big parties. The last regional poll on 14 May 2000 produced a coalition government of SPD (42.8

per cent) and Greens (7.1 per cent). The FDP cleared the electoral hurdle with 9.8 per cent, but the PDS polled what is about the typical result for the western *Länder* – 1.1 per cent.

NRW was well known as (West) Germany's industrial heartland not just for iron and steel, but is still important in the present Federal Republic for the chemical and automobile industries, banking and administration centres, credit and insurance facilities, electronics, brown coal (around Aachen-Düren), textiles and clothing, and machine tools, amongst others. Although its economic restructuring is not yet complete, NRW is still the FRG's strongest *Land* in economic terms, with almost half of the Federal Republic's biggest companies represented there, and over 600,000 small and medium-sized firms.[9]

The NRW constitution was promulgated on 11 July 1950, after the Basic Law had been introduced. It was therefore influenced by and benefited from the democratic, republican and social nature of the West German constitution. With regard to the party system that developed in NRW, in the 13 regional polls there between 1947 and 2000 a trend emerged whereby it went from being a 'CDU federal state' to more of an 'SPD state'.

From 1947 until 1962 the CDU out-polled the SPD in regional contests, even attaining an absolute majority at the 1958 *Landtagswahl*. Yet in 1985 and 1990 it was the SPD under minister president Rau who polled over half the vote. This state of affairs was affected by changes in the SPD direction by the acceptance of the Godesberg programme, and its increasing success in the urban conurbations and predominantly Protestant areas. Their chief rivals of course did best in the predominantly Catholic and rural areas. The Liberals in the service sectors and the Greens gained above-average results in the university towns and big cities.

Like Lower Saxony, North-Rhine Westphalia in local elections used to follow the British model of the *Norddeutsche Ratsverfassung*, using a dual system of electing both an administrator (*Gemeindedirektor*) and a mayor; since 1999 the mayor has been directly chosen for five years by the voters. Local elections in NRW take place every five years and give the voter just one vote.

8.11 Rhineland-Palatinate

The federal state of the Rhineland-Patinate (*Rheinland-Pfalz*) was administered by the French after 1945. Like NRW (see above) it was an artificial creation, though it was originally part of the Prussian Rhine province, strongly orientated towards Cologne and Düsseldorf. In the south the territory to the left of the Rhine used to belong to Bavaria. In the middle of the state the area of Rheinhessen was separated from the state of Hesse. After some years however the new *Land* began to develop its own identity and economic profile. It has borders with Belgium, Luxembourg and France, and is the only German federal state where French, rather than English, is the first foreign language learnt at school. Initially the federal state was a predominantly agricultural one, but it soon took off with wine production (it is estimated some 65 per cent of German wines come from the area), the chemical industry, and supply of wood and car parts. Ceramics, shoes, information technology and broadcasting corporations (ZDF in Mainz and SAT 1) also make a contribution.

The 101-seat *Landtag* in Mainz is elected every five years; each voter has two votes at a regional election and at a local election as many votes as there are places to fill. The Rhineland-Palatinate constitution permits the use of the plebiscite and referendum. In 1975 a referendum was held to ascertain the wishes of the inhabitants of Koblenz, Trier, Montabaur and Rheinhessen vis-à-vis their feeling of identity with the federal state. Their response was positive, and the *Land* has experienced a more integrated feeling of identity ever since.

From 1947 until 1987 deputies in the Rhineland-Palatinate (RP) were chosen from a system of fixed lists in constituencies. In 1992 the Federal Constitutional Court declared the electoral system to be unconstitutional, which led to a correction of the 1971 result. The changes introduced eliminated the way in which the small parties had been disadvantaged. In the 40 years from 1947 the CDU always gained the highest vote and actually received an absolute majority of the seats at six regional contests. Until 1991 the CDU was clearly the dominant political force in RP, where there are more Catholics than Protestants amongst the four million inhabitants, although in the early years the Christian Democrats usually led a coalition with other parties. From 1969 until 1976 Helmut Kohl was the minister president.

At the 1991 regional poll the SPD finally overtook its rivals and chose the FDP as their coalition partner, although the Green Party had the same number of seats. The only other parties which have ever entered parliament in Mainz are the communist KPD in 1947, the DRP (*Deutsche Reichspartei*) in 1959 and the far-right NPD in 1967. At the last *Landtagswahl* on 25 March 2001 the Social Democrats polled nearly 45 per cent against just over 35 per cent for the Christian Democrats, with the Liberals and Alliance 90/the Greens on 7.8 and 5.2 per cent respectively. The social/liberal coalition continued, making RP the only federal state in the FRG currently with an SPD-FDP regional government.

8.12 Saarland

The Saarland occupies a special position amongst Germany's federal states. It is the smallest, after Bremen, with only just over a million inhabitants – a mere 1.3 per cent of the German population. After a splintered and varied history the Saarland, having been annexed from Alsace-Lorraine in 1871, was initially occupied by the American forces in 1945 and then passed over to the French occupation forces. The status of this region of heavy industry (coal and steel) was unclear, as the question of its future (*die Saarfrage*) became a bone of contention between Adenauer and Mendes-France. Finally, in a referendum in October 1955, at which there was a 96.6 per cent turnout, nearly 68 per cent of the citizens of the Saarland voted in favour of returning to Germany. In this way the Saarland became the eleventh *Land* of West Germany on 1 January 1957.

Unfortunately this meant that economic development in the Saarland got off to a rather late start. It was not until 1959 that the Saarland was able to participate properly in the West German economy, and the coal and steel crises of the 1960s and 1970s and growing unemployment left their mark. Between 1960 and 1996 the importance of coal and steel to the local economy was reduced from around 60 per cent to below 25 per cent. Structural change via the areas of energy technology, food stuffs, vehicle production, information technology and tourism was essential. Struggling to master domestic finances and encourage investment is a permanent feature of economic life. Some financial assistance has often been forthcoming via the re-distribution of resources operated by the equalisation of payments (*Länderfinanzausgleich*), a key feature of the German federal system, of which the Saarland has been a regular beneficiary.

In 1947 the occupying forces decided that the regional parliament in Saarbrücken should not contain more than 50 deputies, given the size of the federal state. In 1975 a stalemate situation developed and the number of members of the *Landtag* was increased to 51, simply to avoid future problems in reaching decisions. The legislature is elected for five years, only list seats are permitted, each voter has only one vote at regional elections and no additional mandates are possible. Up until 1985 the CDU dominated politics in the Saarland, sometimes leading government coalitions, but always providing the minister president. In 1985 Oskar Lafontaine (SPD), the former mayor of Saarbrücken, took over and he and the SPD ruled alone, until he became finance minister in the Schröder federal government.

The electoral system for choosing a regional parliament selects 41 deputies from districts (*Kreisverschläge*) and the remaining ten representatives from a statewide list (*Landesvorschläge*). The federal state of Saarland is divided into three constituencies: Saarbrücken, Saarlouis and Neunkirchen. A PR system according to the d'Hondt allocation method is used. Since 1979 the use of the plebiscite and referendum are permitted, but not laws affecting state finance or constitutional amendments. For local polls each voter has one vote in a PR system with fixed lists and full-time mayors and lord mayors are selected from the district councils for a ten-year period of office.

In the period 1946/47 the *Christliche Volkspartei* (CVP) and the *Sozialdemokratische Partei Saar* (SPS) were founded, as well as the *Kommunistische Partei, Landesverband Saar* (KPS). Until 1955 the CVP, under Johannes Hoffmann, dominated the Saarland party system. It was only after the signing of the Franco-German Treaty (Saar statute) in 1955 that these parties disappeared in favour of the mainstream CDU and SPD.

When Lafontaine moved to federal politics, Reinhard Klimmt (SPD) took over as minister president, but a major shock was in store. Firstly Lafontaine resigned very suddenly as federal finance minister on 11 March 1999, and secondly his party, which had come to be very closely linked with Saarland politics, was ejected from power. The last time the Saarland voted for a regional parliament on 5 September 1999 the CDU (45.4 per cent), to the surprise of many, just managed to overtake the SPD (44.4 per cent) and gain one parliamentary seat more than its rivals, making Peter Müller (CDU) the new minister president. All other parties fell well below 5 per cent. This was an unexpected change of power in Saarbrücken.

8.13 Saxony

The Free State of Saxony (*der Freistaat Sachsen*) can look back on a thousand year history. Its established traditions and independent stance stretch back to the year 929 and beyond, when King Henry I built a fortified castle in Meißen and Emperor Otto the Great converted the city into a bishopric and established it as part of the emerging Roman-German empire. The Saxons are one of the oldest Germanic tribes. During the Thirty Years' War Saxony was caught between Prussia and the Hapsburgs. In the nineteenth century the Saxon princes (*Kurfürsten*) were able to call themselves kings and industrial progress came about, as Saxony developed into one of the most innovative and modern economic centres in Germany. On 10 November 1918 a workers and soldiers council took over in Dresden and proclaimed a Republic (the term Free State, was a synonym for Republic).

Following the collapse of the Berlin Wall and the GDR in 1989/90, the Free State of Saxony was re-established with the fourth constitution in its history on 6 June 1992. It placed great emphasis on respect for basic human rights. Although the political history of Saxony, and its present-day capital of Dresden, had always furthered the cause of social democracy, at the first post German Unity elections on 14 October 1990, as in other former GDR areas, a CDU majority was established. This was no doubt influenced by the fact that it was a CDU-led government in Bonn, under the leadership of Kohl as the 'father of German unity' that was associated with a united Germany. Kurt Biedenkopf, born in Chemnitz but basically a West German politician with long experience with the Christian Democrats in North-Rhine Westphalia, moved to the east and took over as CDU minister president. Administrative changes were made, in order to simplify the overall structure. The 48 districts (*Landkreise*) were reduced to 22, plus seven independent cities (*kreisfreie Städte*), which were set up in Chemnitz, Dresden, Görlitz, Hoyerswerda, Leipzig, Plauen and Zwickau.

Nowadays Saxony, with close to 4.5 million inhabitants, is often regarded as the most significant and successful of the eastern *Länder*. As in most of the eastern states, there are very few foreigners in Saxony. Dresden, Leipzig and Chemnitz, with populations of just under half a million, just over half a million and about 270,000 respectively, are important centres for business and the service industries.

Saxony has been governed by the CDU since 1990, and at the most recent regional poll there on 19 September 1999 the CDU gained an absolute majority of the vote (56.9 per cent), the PDS polled over 20 per cent (22.4), and the SPD only just cleared 10 per cent (10.7). Biedenkopf was re-elected minister president yet again, but he stood down in May 2002, when Georg Milbradt (CDU) took over. The *Landtag* in Dresden contains 120 deputies, half of whom are elected via constituencies and the other half via fixed party lists for a five-year period of office. At local contests in Saxony each voter has up to three votes at his or her disposal. This allows for the possibility of *kumulieren* (giving more than one vote to a candidate) and *panaschieren* (voting for candidates from different party lists). The voting system is based on PR with open lists, and local mayors are chosen for periods of office which may vary according to the local situation, but is often between five and seven years. There is some variety too in the party representation of mayors: whilst the conservative capital of Dresden has a CDU mayor, the SPD was successful in Leipzig and Chemnitz, and Hoyerswerda has a *Bürgermeister* from the PDS.

8.14 Saxony-Anhalt

The federal state of Saxony-Anhalt (*Sachsen-Anhalt*) has long historical traditions in both a German and a European context. Although much of the surrounding territory has more than one thousand years of history, the actual *Land* itself is a comparatively new entity. It was created in 1945 by a command from the Soviet occupation forces, out of the former Prussian province of Saxony, the Free State of Anhalt and parts of Brunswick (*Braunschweig*) and Thuringia. As with the other East German federal states, Saxony-Anhalt became one of the *Lander* of the GDR until they were dissolved in favour of the new administrative districts (*Bezirke*) in 1952. In 1990 the federal state was re-established, along with, after lengthy discussions, its capital Magdeburg.

With its 2.7 million inhabitants, this is a federal state that has experienced a lot of problems since 1990. Unemployment has always been, and still is, higher in the east than in the west of Germany, but it has often reached a peak in Saxony-Anhalt (SA). In June 2002, for example, the unemployment rate in the other eastern states was between 15.8 and 17.9 per cent, yet it was 19.8 per cent in SA. In the west it was much lower, with only 5.1 per cent unemployed in Baden-Württemberg and 5.5 per cent in Bavaria. All the western federal states had single figure percentages, with only Bremen at 12.5 per cent. In terms of GDP, the *Land* of SA usually records the lowest growth. Its economy is now aimed at the production of motor vehicles, machinery, foodstuffs, chemicals and energy production, but it was over-dependent on agriculture for many years.

Following German Unity, SA was organised around three towns/cities (*kreisfreie Städte*) – Magdeburg, Halle and Dessau – and after the land reform of 1 July 1994 it was divided into 21, instead of 37, districts (*Landkreise*). Many economic and environmental problems needed to be addressed. The pollution around the area of Bitterfeld was only one of difficulties.

SA's first *Land* government after 1990 was a CDU/FDP coalition. From 1994 onwards Reinhard Höppner (SPD) led a SPD/Green minority coalition government, tolerated by the PDS (the CDU tried to run a 'red socks' (*rote Socken*) campaign against the Social Democrats. The CDU suffered great losses in their support in 1998, and Alliance 90/the Greens failed to clear 5 per cent, as has often happened in the eastern states. However, at the last regional election in SA on 21 April 2002 the CDU recovered to take over 37 per cent of the vote, and the FDP recorded a staggering 13.3 per cent; the state parliament in Magdeburg is now governed by a conservative/liberal coalition government. This means that SA is the only federal state in the east where the

Free Democrats are part of the government. In 2002 the SPD and the PDS polled 20 and 20.4 per cent respectively, with Alliance 90/the Greens managing only 2 per cent. Saxony-Anhalt is the only exception at present to the rule of the western states having a four-party system (two big parties and two small ones) and the eastern states having a three-party system (PDS, SPD, CDU).

Regional elections in Saxony Anhalt are held every four years and each voter has two votes. One deputy is selected from each of the forty-nine constituencies; a minimum of a further fifty members of the Magdeburg parliament are chosen via the second vote, making a total of at least ninety-nine deputies. However, this number can be, and often is, increased, owing to the provision of a balancing mechanism (*Ausgleichsmandate*). At local elections in Sachsen-Anhalt each voter has three votes and, in line with a number of other federal states, the voting age has been reduced from eighteen to sixteen.

8.15 Schleswig-Holstein

The northern state of Schleswig-Holstein (SH) acts as a territorial bridge between central Europe (northern Germany) and the peninsula of Scandinavia. There were many disputes and bloody battles over the border with Denmark over many hundreds of years. The position of the border was not finally fixed until the Treaty of Versailles. In 1920 a referendum was held, and ever since there has been a German minority living north of the border and a Danish minority living south of the border. The Danish minority living in Germany is represented by its own 'protected' political party (see below).

With just under 2.8 million inhabitants occupying the territory between the North Sea and the Baltic, the federal state of SH consists of three geographical regions, covering marsh land, coastal moor lands and hilly terrain. There is a long history of struggles amongst the Franks, Friesians, Danes and Slavs battling over land here, some of which go back to the eighth century. Today the population of SH still contains two significant minorities: some 50,000 Danes and some 160,000 Friesians. Approximately 100,000 of the latter speak Friesian, which is recognised as a separate European language for communication, and is not classified as a dialect, such as Low German (*Plattdeutsch*).

In terms of the economy, SH is moving from one which was traditionally based mainly on agriculture, shipping (particularly around the state capital Kiel) and fishing, to one associated with modern industry, manufacturing and the service sector. Tourism is important too and trade via the ports of Kiel and Lübeck is increasing again with the widening access to the eastern territories.

The population is predominantly Protestant. The first regional elections in 1947, held under the aegis of the British occupation forces, were won by the SPD. From 1950 until 1988, however, the CDU ruled and dominated the political development of SH, either ruling alone or in coalition with the other parties. There were several of these that were strongly represented. They included the party of Refugees and Expellees (BHE), which in 1950 gained more votes than the CDU and was only slightly behind the SPD, the DP (*Deutsche Partei*), the FDP and the SSW (*Südschleswigscher Wählerverband*). The SSW is the party representing the Danish minority and it does not have to clear the 5 per cent barrier. It is guaranteed representation in the *Landtag*. For all the other parties in SH the alternative to gaining at least 5 per cent of the valid second votes at a regional election is winning one direct constituency seat. The split between constituency and list seats is normally 45/30, making a total of 75 deputies in the *Landtag* in Kiel, which is elected every four years. Each voter at a regional contest has one vote.

From 1988 onwards the SPD took over in SH, winning a massive majority after the notorious and unsavoury Barschel Affair. That was the most scandalous political affair in SH in the postwar period; it has never been completely forgotten there. The CDU minister president Uwe Barschel was allegedly involved in electoral sharp practices and later found dead in a Geneva hotel room in 1987. Originally both murder and suicide were suspected. In 1988 Björn Engholm (SPD) took over as minister president with an absolute majority. He was victorious again in 1992, but had to stand down five years later, when it came to light that he had actually been more involved in the political scandal than was originally known, although at the time Engholm was the one being smeared.

In 1993 Heide Simonis (SPD) took over the leadership of SH and became the first female minister president in the Federal Republic. From 1996 onwards she formed a government coalition with the Greens. A red/green coalition also continued, following the most recent regional elections on 27 February 2000, at which the SPD received just over 43 per cent of the vote and the CDU just over 35 per cent. The PDS gained just over 1 per cent – a typical figure for a western state – and the SSW was allocated three parliamentary seats in Kiel, even though it recorded only 4.1 per cent. The 5 per cent hurdle does not apply to the SSW, representing the Danish minority (see above).

At local elections in SH, normally held every four years, the voter has as many votes as there are direct mandates to be allocated. It is an unusual voting method, compared with the methods used in other German states at local polls, since it consists of a two-stage process, with a majority system in single or multiple constituencies, combined with a PR fixed list system acting as a balancing mechanism. The mayors in SH are directly elected by the voters for a period of office of between six and eight years.

8.16 Thuringia

The Free State of Thuringia (*der Freistaat Thüringen*) is small, both in terms of geographical size and population density. With less than two-and-a-half million inhabitants, and the smallest percentage of non-Germans than any of the 16 federal states, Thuringia is sometimes known as 'the green heart of Germany' (*das grüne Herz Deutschlands*), because it has so many forests – around one third of its area is woodland. Consequently this area has a long tradition of tourism, owing to the scenic attractions of its forests (*der Thüringer Wald*).

The economy of Thuringia has undergone significant development since 1990. Agriculture was always important, but it was strengthened further, building on the LPG cooperatives of the former GDR. The main established university in Jena, the newly founded university in Erfurt and the technical university in Ilmenau are involved in research and computer related industries. Enterprises connected with motor manufacture (BMW, General Motors) have been established in Eisenach and optical instruments in Jena have been promoted. The situation in terms of economic development is now more favourable. Nevertheless, unemployment remains stubbornly high, as is of course still the case in the eastern *Länder* generally, and the situation vis-à-vis the western federal states has to be seen in a different light.

After Thuringia joined the new Germany, via article 23 of the Basic Law, the first regional elections were held in October 1990. They produced a result of over 45 per cent for the CDU, nearly 23 per cent for the SPD, under 10 per cent for the PDS and the same for the FDP, and under 7 per cent for the Greens. CDU-FDP coalition government was formed in Erfurt, led by Josef Duchac (CDU). In 1992 Duchac stepped down, however, having lost the confidence of his colleagues; the former CDU minister president of the Rhineland-Palatinate, Bernhard Vogel, took over the reigns of power in Thuringia and has retained that position until the present. Vogel currently presides over a government ruled by the Christian Democrats alone, since their last victory on 12 September 1999, at which the CDU gained an absolute majority, the PDS 21.3 per cent, and the SPD 18.5 per cent. All other parties fell at the 5 per cent hurdle. That meant that at present the party system in Thuringia conforms to the general, though not only, pattern in the eastern states: it is namely a three-party system (CDU, SPD, PDS).

The Erfurt parliament normally consists of 88 deputies (44 from the constituencies, and 44 from the party lists) and gives the voter two votes in a regional election, based on PR and the Hare/Nieyer allocation procedure. *Landtagswahlen* are held every five years and *Kommunalwahlen* every four years. In local polls the electoral system used in Thuringia is very similar to that of Schleswig-Holstein (see above).

Notes

1   Hans-Georg Wehling (ed.) (2000), *Die deutschen Länder. Geschichte, Politik, Wirtschaft*, Opladen: Leske und Budrich, p. 25.

2   For a fuller account of the history and development see the chapter on Berlin by Sue Lawson in Peter James (ed.) (1998), *Modern Germany. Politics, Society and Culture*, London and New York: Routledge.

3   See Joanna Mackay's article 'Berlin-Brandenburg? Nein danke!', in *German Politics*, Vol. 5, No. 3.

4   'Berlin ist keine Wirtschaftsmetropole', Hansjoachim Hoffmann's chapter 'Berlin. Bundesland und wieder Hauptstadt', p. 79 in Hans-Georg Wehling, op. cit.

5   See article 'Drei Hessen unter einem Hut', by Elisabeth Abendroth and Klaus Böhme in Hans-Georg Wehling, op. cit.

6   See Uwe Andersen and Wichard Woyke (eds) (1997), *Handbuch des politischen Systems der BRD*, Bonn: Bundeszentrale für politische Bildung, p. 298.

7   See Dan Hough (2003), 'It's the East, Stupid. Eastern Germany and the Outcome of the 2002 Bundestagswahl', an article in *Representation*, Vol. 39, No. 2, p. 141.

8   Ibid., p. 145, note 1.

9   Referred to in Andreas Kost, 'Nordrhein-Westfalen. Vom Land aus der Retorte zum 'Wir-Gefühl', p. 179 in Hans-Georg Wehling, op. cit.

Chapter 9

Conclusion

As we saw at the beginning of this book, the current German electoral system evolved from, and was influenced by, voting methods used in political systems in Germany's past. That is particularly relevant to the Weimar Republic. Following the political chaos that reared its head between 1919 and 1933, which was not caused by – but neither was it helped by – the electoral system of pure PR with no cut-off clause, stringent efforts were made to learn the appropriate lessons by the 'fathers' of the Basic Law. Although the details of the electoral system were not contained in the *Grundgesetz* itself (electoral laws were issued subsequently), the West German system of 'personalised PR', which had developed by 1956, was considerably influenced by a desire to avoid the pitfalls of some of the 'unfair' and disproportionate election results of the Prussian and Second Empire systems. The introduction in 1949 of the 5 per cent clause was certainly a direct reaction to the Weimar experience, where the shortcomings of pure PR in practice had been in evidence for all to see.

Although there are many different electoral systems in existence throughout the world, the decision taken in the period 1945–49 for the new post-war liberal parliamentary democracy about to be established was between two fundamentally different systems, each with a different effect on the political system. As has been shown, a majority voting system is normally more likely to lead to the establishment of an alternating two-party system, of the type which exists today in the UK and the USA. A proportional system, on the other hand, like the one adopted for the Federal Republic of Germany, is normally more likely to produce a multi-party system, making the formation of coalition governments involving two or more parties and consensus more probable.

In the case of Germany, the application of the new electoral system to the results of the first federal election in 1949 did produce what looked like the beginnings of a multiparty system. By means of the tightening of the electoral hurdle and other amendments, the voting system proved itself to be sufficiently flexible to adapt to developments. Following the federal contests of 1953, 1957 and 1961 six, four and three parties respectively entered the *Bundestag* in Bonn. Between 1961 and 1983 the West German electoral system continued to be successful in providing the stability in electoral politics which the new republic had so desperately sought after the chaotic and negative experiences of Weimar and National Socialism.

When a new phenomenon, in the shape of the Green Party, arrived on the West German political stage at federal level in 1983, the electoral system, as an essential component of the polity of the FRG, enabled a four-party system to function equally well. The Greens were an example of a political movement that was able to build up slowly from the grassroots level, at first locally, then regionally, before surmounting the electoral barrier at federal level. Indeed, as we have seen, the new party of Alliance 90/the Greens, formed in 1993, has now twice been able to offer its services as a government coalition partner in the federal parliament.

It has also been demonstrated in this book that the German electoral system, as a key element in the political system, has proved itself more than capable of withstanding pressures placed on it. In 1956 there was a strong move to change to a majority system; this came originally from Adenauer and the CDU/CSU, who had become impatient with their FDP partners, especially over the Saar question. Although Adenauer and his Christian Democrats managed to gain an absolute majority of the vote in the 1957 federal poll and rule without the Free Democrats, the electoral system was in fact not changed, and it continued to function viably.

The criticism has of course been made from time to time that the tiny FDP was able, for many years, to adopt roles and functions in the party system of the Federal Republic which were disproportionate to its size, mainly as a result of an electoral system based on PR that encouraged the formation of coalition governments, of which the Free Democrats were so often a member. A check on the number of cabinet ministers in government over the years quickly reveals that the power and influence of the Liberals was far greater than their numbers in terms of party membership and electoral support merited. Given the nature of Germany's 'personalised proportional' system, which is likely to lead to coalition governments, often consisting of one large and one small partner, this situation was to a certain extent inevitable. The functions of the FDP in the party system of the FRG – above all in West Germany, but also in the period 1990–98, after German Unity – disappeared when the Schröder/ Fischer red-green federal governments of 1998 and 2002 took over.

As we saw in the Introduction, various experts writing about German politics see the electoral system as being central to the shaping of the political system itself, whilst others view the political system as being influential in shaping the electoral system. Clearly the two are intertwined. The type of parties which emerge and prosper in a national polity, and also the nature of that polity itself can, and will, have an effect on the electoral system. Equally the latter will influence the party system. There seems little doubt that this has been the case in the Federal Republic. Most experts would agree that the German electoral system, first designed for a 'provisional' state that was desperately seeking to establish a stable parliamentary democracy in the late 1940s has stood the test of time.

Appendices

Appendix A: Results of the federal elections 1949–2002

Year	Turnout %	CDU/ CSU	SPD	FDP	Greens	PDS	Seat total
1949	78.5	31.0	29.2	11.9	–	–	402
1953	85.8	45.2	28.8	9.5	–	–	487
1957	87.8	50.2	318	7.7	–	–	497
1961	87.7	45.3	36.2	12.8	–	–	499
1965	86.8	47.6	39.3	9.5	–	–	496
1969	86.7	46.1	42.7	5.8	–	–	496
1972	91.1	44.9	45.8	8.4	–	–	496
1976	90.7	48.6	42.6	7.9	–	–	496
1980	88.6	44.5	42.9	10.6	1.5	–	497
1983	89.1	48.8	38.2	7.0	5.6	–	498
1987	84.3	44.3	37.0	9.1	8.3	–	497
1990	77.8	43.8	33.5	11.0	3.8	2.4	662
1994	79.0	41.4	36.4	6.9	7.3	4.4	672
1998	82.3	35.2	40.9	6.2	6.7	5.1	669
2002	79.1	38.5	38.5	7.4	8.6	4.0	603

Appendix B: Population, denomination and manual workers in the German *Länder*

Land	Population (million)	% R. Catholic	% Protestant	% manual workers	% foreigners
Baden-Würt.	10.47	40	42	35	13
Bavaria	12.1	64	24	34	9
Berlin	3.38	13	61	27	13
Brandenburg	2.6	4	68	38	2
Bremen	0.67	10	62	34	11
Hamburg	1.7	7	53	25	15
Hesse	6.0	25	56	31	12
Lower Saxony	7.9	20	59	35	12
Meck-Pom.	1.78	5	24	42	2
NRW	18.0	48	35	33	11
Rh-Palatinate	4.0	52	34	36	8
Saarland	1.07	68	23	36	8
Saxony	4.46	4	30	44	2
Sax.-Anhalt	2.6	5	26	43	2
Schl.-Holstein	2.77	6	65	29	6
Thuringia	2.45	9	34	41	2
Germany	82.2	34	38	35	9
Western states		41	41	33	
Eastern states		5	28	41	

Source: adapted from various tables in Bundestagswahl (2002), *Eine Analyse der Wahl vom 22*, September, Mannheim: Berichte der Forschungsgruppe Wahlen e.V., No. 108.

Bibliography

Albrecht, B. et al. (2002), *Der Fischer Weltalmanach 2003*, Frankfurt: Fischer Taschenbuch Verlag.

Andersen, U. and Woyke, W. (ed.) (1997), *Handwörterbuch des politischen Systems der BRD*, Bonn: Bundeszentrale für politische Bildung.

Backes, U. and Moreau, P. (1993), *Die extreme Rechte in Deutschland*, Munich: Akademischer Verlag.

Beier, B. et al. (1983), *Die Chronik der Deutschen*, Dortmund: Chronik Verlag/Harenberg.

Brauntal, G. (1996), *Parties and Politics in Modern Germany*, Colorado and Oxford: Westview Press.

Bundestagswahl 1998 (1998), Mannheim: Forschungsgruppe Wahlen e.V.

Bundestagswahl 2002 (2002), Mannheim: Forschungsgruppe Wahlen e.V.

Burkett, T. and Padgett, S. (1986), *Political Parties and Elections in West Germany*, London: Hurst.

Conradt, D. (2001), *The German Polity*, 7th edn, New York: Longman.

Der Spiegel, 29 September 2002, *Wahlsonderheft '02*.

Edinger, L. (1986), *West German Politics*, New York: Columbia University Press.

German Politics, Journal of the Association for the Study of German Politics, various.

Hamm-Brücher, H. (1981), *Vorkämpfer für Demokratie und Gerechtigkeit in Bayern und Bonn*, Bonn: Liberal-Verlag.

Hough, D. (2003), 'It's the East, Stupid! Eastern Germany and the Outcome of the 2002 Bundstagswahl', *Representation*, Vol. 39, No. 2.

Hübner, E. (1978), *Wahlsysteme*, Munich: Bayerische Landeszentrale für politische Bildung.

James, P. (1995), *The Politics of Bavaria – An Exception to the Rule*, Aldershot and Brookfield: Avebury.

James, P. (ed.) (1998), *Modern Germany: Politics, Society and Culture*, London and New York: Routledge.

James, P. (2003), 'The 2002 German Federal Election – The "Fotofinish"', *Representation*, Vol. 39, No. 2.

Jeffery, C. (1999), *Recasting German Federalism: The Legacies of Unification*, London: Pinter.

Jeffery, C. and Whittle, R. (1997), *Germany Today*, London, New York, Sydney, Auckland: Arnold.

Jüttner, A. (1970), *Wahlen und Wahlrechtsprobleme*, Munich: Olzog.

Katzenstein, P. (1987), *Policy and Politics in West Germany: The Growth of a Semi-Sovereign State*, Philadelphia: Temple University Press.

Korte, K.-R. (1998), *Wahlen in der BRD*, Bonn: Bundeszentrale für politische Bildung.

Korte, K.-R. (2000), *Wahlen in der BRD*, Bonn: Bundeszentrale für politische Bildung.

Lange, E. (1975), *Wahlrecht und Innenpolitik 1945–56*, Meisenheim am Glan: Anton Hain Verlag.

Laufer, H. (1991), *Das föderative System der BRD*, Munich: Bayerische Landeszentrale für politische Bildungsarbeit.

Lösche, P. and Walter, F. (1996), *Die FDP*, Darmstadt: Wissenschaftliche Buchgesellschaft.

Milatz, A. (1965), *Wähler und Wahlen in der Weimarer Republik*, Bonn: Bundeszentrale für politische Bildung.

Mintzel, A. (1977), *Geschichte der CSU*, Opladen: Westdeutscher Verlag.

Mintzel, A. and Oberreuter, H. (1992), *Parteien in der BRD*, Opladen: Leske und Buddrich.

Nohlen, D. (1978), *Wahlsysteme der Welt. Daten und Analyse. Ein Handbuch*, Munich: Piper.

Nohlen, D. (2000), *Wahlrecht und Parteiensystem*, 3rd edn, Opladen: Westdeutscher Verlag.

Padgett, S. and Saalfeld, T. (1994), *Parties and Party Systems in the New Germany*, Aldershot and Brookfield: Dartmouth.

Parkes, S. (1997), *Understanding Contemporary Germany*, London and New York: Routledge.

Paterson, W. (1985), 'The Christian Union Parties', in Wallach, H.G.P. and Rohrmoser, G.K. (eds), *West German Politics in the Mid-Eighties*, New York: Praeger.

Paterson, W. and Southern, D. (1991), *Governing Germany*, Oxford: Blackwell.

Politbarometer, various reports compiled by Forschungsgruppe Wahlen, Mannheim.

Pukelsheim, F. (2000), M'andatszuteilungen bei Verhältniswahlen: Erfolgswertgleichheit der Wählerstimmen', *Rundschau/News and Reports*, Physik-Verlag.

Pulzer, P. (1995), *German Politics 1945–95*, Oxford: Oxford University Press.

Roberts, G. (1996), 'The Great Escape: the EDP and the Superwahljahr', in Dalton, R. (ed.), *Germans Divided. The 1994 Bundestag Elections and the Evolution of the German Party System*, Oxford: Berg.

Roberts, G. (2000), *German Politics Today*, Manchester and New York: Manchester University Press.

Roth, D. (1998), *Empirische Wahlforschung*, Opladen: Leske und Budrich.

Rudzio, W. (2001), *Das politische System der BRD*, Hagen: Polis.

Schmidt, M. (2003), *Political Institutions in the FRG*, Oxford and New York: Oxford University Press.

Siaroff, A. (2000), 'British AMS versus German Personalised PR: Not So Different', *Representation*, Vol. 37, No.1, Summer.

Smith, G. (1979), *Democracy in Western Germany: Parties and Politics in the Federal Republic*, London: Heinemann.

Smith, G., Paterson, W. and Padgett, S. (eds) (1996), *Developments in German Politics 2*, Basingstoke: Macmillan.

Urwin, D. (1974), 'Germany', in Rose, R. (ed.), *Electoral Behaviour: A Comparative Handbook*, New York: Macmillan.

Watson, A. (1995), *The Germans: Who Are They Now?*, London: Mandarin.

Wehling, H.-G. (ed.) (2000), *Die deutschen Länder. Geschichte, Politik, Wirtschaft*, Opladen: Leske und Budrich.

World Report on Germany, *Financial Times*, 25 November 2002.

Index

Note: bold page numbers indicate tables and illustrations.